THE ULTIMATE
RIBBON
BOOK

VV ROULEAUX

THE ULTIMATE
RIBBON
BOOK

ANNABEL LEWIS

PHOTOGRAPHY BY PIA TRYDE

Trafalgar Square Publishing

For Richard, Phoebe, Fanny, Monty and Tallulah

First published in the
United States of America in 1995 by
Trafalgar Square Publishing,
North Pomfret, Vermont 05053

Printed in China

First published in Great Britain in 1995 by
Conran Octopus Limited
37 Shelton Street
London WC2H 9HN

Library of Congress Catalog Card Number: 95-60031

ISBN 1-57076-030-6

Art Editor & Photographic Art Direction Georgina Rhodes
Project Editor Tessa Clayton
Stylist Julia Bird
Commissioning Editor Louise Simpson
Production Mano Mylvaganam
Picture Researcher Rachel Davies
Illustrations Ian Sidaway
Typesetting Richard Proctor

Produced by Mandarin Offset Ltd

CONTENTS

INTRODUCTION

HISTORY

Ribbons are one of the oldest forms of adornment. As far back as the Middle Ages, Chaucer's tales refer to 'ribbands' – narrow bands of fabric used to edge and trim garments. During the medieval and Renaissance periods, however, ribbons were often woven with gold and silver thread, making them an expensive luxury. There was even an Act of Parliament in the sixteenth century which sought to restrict the wearing of ribbons to all but the nobility.

By the late seventeenth century, however, the demand for ribbons had increased tenfold. At this time, fashions in clothing and home furnishings veered towards the extravagant, and both men's and women's outfits and accessories – shoes, gloves, waistbands, gowns and bonnets – were adorned with ornate ribbon rosettes and frills. Similarly, soft furnishings such as curtains and cushions, often already elaborately patterned, were further embellished with broad stripes of ruched silk ribbon. In response to this growing demand for high-quality ribbons, merchants and weavers already involved in the silk industry saw a chance to expand their interests, and centres devoted to ribbon production began to spring up, most notably in Lyons in France and Coventry in England.

The fledgling industry flourished. The silk merchants bought raw silk from the Continent and passed it on to middlemen, who boiled, cleaned, twisted and dyed the yarn. The ribbons were then painstakingly woven on hand-operated looms, before being despatched to shops in London and abroad.

After 1770, new technological break-throughs such as the Dutch Engine Loom, capable of producing up to six ribbons at a time, greatly improved productivity. Ribbons were as much in demand as ever, with the fashionable ladies of the day clamouring for ribbons to decorate the elaborate towering wigs that were in vogue. In contrast, in America, very little ribbon was worn – possibly as a deliberate stand against the extravagance of the English court.

The first major set-back for the ribbon trade came with the Napoleonic wars in the early nineteenth century, when many skilled weavers were recruited into the army. With the demand for ribbons as great as ever, the smuggling of French ribbons became rife. The wars did little to quench the public's thirst for new fashions, and innovative ribbon designs were much sought after. In 1813, a craze for the purl-edge, or picot-edge – a ribbon with delicately scalloped sides – took the industry by storm. The demand

FAR RIGHT:
MARIE-ANTOINETTE (Louise Elisabeth Vigeé-Lebrun, 1755-1842). *No eighteenth-century dress was complete without a host of ornate ribbon bows and knots.*

RIGHT, ABOVE & BELOW:
Not just fashionable fripperies, ribbons have long had a ceremonial role. During the nineteenth century, military knitted tapes and jacquards were used to embellish regimental uniforms, and medal ribbons are still in use today.

was so great that weavers could ask virtually any price for their wares. The enormous production of purl-edge ribbons lasted for another two years, until the fashion died out as quickly as it had arrived, and the industry moved on to service yet another trend. These waves of popularity in ribbon design were affected by different events, such as deaths in the royal family, when there would be a demand for black accessories.

During the Victorian era, however, new European trade agreements made it increasingly difficult for English ribbons to compete with Continental imports, and despite using cheap female labour and investing in larger, more automated, looms, many manufacturers suffered.

Though ribbons would never again dominate the fashions of the day, the ribbon trade was not completely decimated. The more astute manufacturers diversified, and adapted their looms to weave fringes, braids, silk pictures and bookmarks, as well as the military medal ribbons, tapes and braids that decorated the regimental uniforms of the day.

I have discovered the most amazing ribbons – both antique and modern – in my travels at home and abroad, and brought back delicate organdies, thick cotton tapes, smooth, glossy satins and pleated grosgrains, to mention just a few, to my London shop, V V Rouleaux. This passion for ribbon has been an adventure for me, and I learn something new and exciting every day. I hope this book will communicate some of that excitement, and demonstrate – through myriad projects for beribboned furnishings, clothing, ornaments and gifts – both the beauty and the versatility of ribbons.

Annabel Lewis

CHOOSING RIBBONS

With the vast array of ribbons now available, choosing the right ribbon for your needs can seem a daunting prospect. Modern ribbons come in every imaginable texture – from rich and lustrous velvets to the sheerest, translucent organdies – and every conceivable hue, from solid colours through to vibrant stripes, polka-dots and tartans, or subtly-shaded ombrés. Ribbon widths can vary from narrow (3mm/¹⁄₈in) to broad (up to 150mm/6in). And ribbons can be given any number of special finishes: appliquéd, flocked or embroidered patterns; scalloped or wire edges.

The projects in this book make use of a wide variety of different ribbon types to create Christmas and wedding decorations, trimmings for upholstery and soft furnishings, and embellishments for hats and clothing. Where appropriate, each project recommends a ribbon type to use – hardwearing ribbon for practical items that will be subjected to wear and tear; softer, more delicate ribbons for embellishments and decorative purposes – but more often you will be free to experiment with the ribbons of your choice. You will find helpful advice on choosing ribbons overleaf, and samples of over 200 gloriously coloured ribbons in the glossary on pp.102-113, to provide you with all the design inspiration you need.

RIBBON MANUFACTURE

Ribbons fall into three main categories:

CUT-EDGE

Cut-edge ribbons (also known as craft ribbons) are produced by cutting broad pieces of fabric into strips of varying widths. The fabric, often ready-patterned or with a foil-printed or heat-transferred design, is treated with a special stiffening agent which prevents the cut edges of the ribbon from fraying. Because of the simplicity of the manufacturing process, cut-edge ribbons are relatively inexpensive, though most cannot be washed.

WOVEN-EDGE

Ribbons woven as narrow strips of fabric, with two selvedge edges. These edges can be straight, or more elaborately shaped, giving a picot (scalloped) effect. Most woven-edge ribbons are washable, making them suitable for decorating clothing and soft furnishings.

WIRE-EDGE

Wire-edge ribbons are manufactured in one of two ways: wide ribbons are cut from broadcloth and then have wire edges overlocked along their sides, or fine copper wire is woven in along the sides (or sometimes the centre) of the ribbon during the weaving process. Ribbons can also be made almost entirely from wire mesh, with small additional quantities of silk or metallic yarn. Flexible and malleable, wire-edge and wire mesh ribbons are ideal for moulding into elaborate bows and will hold their shape indefinitely. The majority, however, cannot be washed.

RIBBON TEXTURES

Ribbons are produced from an incredible range of yarns and fibres. Some of the best known ribbon textures include:

GROSGRAINS

Ribbed woven ribbons, usually created from a blend of cotton and viscose, or sometimes polyester, yarns. Strong and hard-wearing, grosgrains were traditionally used by milliners to decorate hats and bonnets. Now available in a wide range of finishes: appliquéd, patterned, picot-edged or pleated.

METALLICS

Popular choices for sparkling festive decorations, gift wrapping and packaging, metallics can either be cut-edge or woven from lurex or other metallic yarns.

VELVETS

Velvet ribbons have a luxurious soft pile, usually on one side only, but occasionally on both sides. Available in single colours, with printed or flocked patterns, pleated, wire-edged or satin-backed.

ORGANDIES

Diaphanous ribbons, made from very finely woven yarns, organdies are incredibly light and delicate in appearance. Often manufactured with a thicker woven or wire edge, organdies can be pleated, interlaced with metallic fibres, appliquéd or embroidered, or patterned with printed or woven designs.

SATINS

Never out of fashion, satins have a unique gloss that makes them an ever-popular choice for gift wrapping, packaging, decorations, and embellishing hairstyles and clothing. They can be single-face – shiny on one side only – or double-face, with two shiny sides, and are available in single colours, with woven or printed patterns, or finished with delicate picot edges. In recent years, manufacturers have been introducing more wire-edge satins onto the market.

NATURAL FIBRES

As well as being woven from man-made yarns, ribbons are also manufactured from a wide range of natural fibres, most notably paper, cotton and linen. Paper ribbons range from the simplest strips cut from broad rolls of strengthened paper, to elaborate scalloped-edged ribbons, or 'paper lace' decorated with intricate cut-out designs. Bolduc, traditionally

used by French pâtissiers *to decorate cakes and pastries, is a narrow ribbon made by fusing together long strands of cotton fibres. Look out also for narrow cotton tapes in a wide range of colours, thick ribbons woven from jute and cotton, linen ribbons, and paper ribbons decorated with foil-printed designs.*

JACQUARDS

First developed in France in the late eighteenth century, jacquards are ribbons woven with elaborate or intricate designs. More costly to manufacture than ordinary woven or cut-edge ribbons, many jacquards are still imported from France, where they are woven on traditional looms (though the use of computerized looms is gradually becoming more widespread).

KEY

1 Wire mesh metallic

2 Foil-print paper

3 Grosgrain

4 Woven-edge organdy

5 Embroidered organdy

6 Double-face satin

7 Cut edge

8 Jacquard

9 Overlocked wire edge

10 Pleated velvet

11 Metallic

RIBBONS & WRAPS

RIBBONS & WRAPS

Today's hectic lifestyles leave little room for us to indulge our creative impulses. Rushing out at the eleventh hour for shop-bought birthday cakes and wrapping paper is a scenario that most of us are all too familiar with, and we are often left regretting that we couldn't spend a little more time, and lavish a little extra attention, on gifts for our loved ones.

Ribbon trimmings are the ideal way to give your handiwork a personal touch without taking up inordinate amounts of time. Whether it be topping an iced cake with ribbon roses to make a tea-time treat extra special *(see p.27)* or customizing your stationery with tiny gold bows *(left)*, decorating with ribbons takes no time at all, and is simple enough for anyone to try. Why not recruit the children to help? Cut a piece of wire netting and let them thread bright ribbons through the mesh to make a useful storage rack for their bedroom or playroom *(see pp.28-9)*.

Half the fun is in finding out what works and what doesn't, so don't be over-cautious. Wrap birthday gifts with a few faded pages from an old book, and bind with claret or dark blue velvet bows. As you move on to new projects, you can use all your left-over ribbon scraps in a host of inventive ways, such as turning snippets of checked, spotted and striped ribbon into tiny flags to decorate a fairy-tale castle of a cake *(see pp.24-5)*.

You'll soon discover that ribbon trimmings can also give old or faded items a new lease of life. Rescue dog-eared books or scruffy leather-bound blotters with a few deft cosmetic touches and trim corners with Butterfly Pleats made from folded gingham ribbon *(see p.22)*. Once you've mastered this simple technique, use it to decorate any number of surfaces – try pillows, cushions, place mats, even lampshades. You don't have to follow the projects in this chapter letter for letter; there are no rules that say that any one ribbon type should be used for any one purpose, so experiment with different colours and textures.

And if you're feeling unambitious, just remember that a single gloriously coloured ribbon can work wonders. There is such an amazing range of ribbons to plunder, from sparkling metallics to gossamer-fine, translucent organdies, that even the simplest of bows will transform a plain parcel into a beautifully wrapped gift, or a simple posy into a lavish bouquet. The more familiar you become with basic ribbon-craft techniques and the types of ribbon available, the more exciting you will find the possibilities for creating your own unique designs.

PREVIOUS PAGES:

Luxurious ribbon textures contrast with rough-edged parchment paper and add a touch of elegance to even the plainest stationery.

LEFT:

For really special love letters, make tiny slots in letter-heads and envelopes, feed through short lengths of beautiful satin-edge gold taffeta, and tie into bows. There are endless variations for different occasions: try tartan ribbon for an engagement announcement, or rich red double-face satin for a ruby wedding anniversary.

SMART STATIONERY IDEAS

PARCHMENT FOLDER

*This beribboned folder is a more
stylish home for old bills, letters
and notes than a scruffy plastic
wallet or the kitchen drawer. To
make it, cut two pieces of thick
card to the same size, and cover
with parchment paper or
wallpaper. Bind together by
gluing a stiff and hard-wearing
millinery petersham ribbon
down the 'spine'.*

*For the ribbon ties, cut two
narrow strips of grosgrain
ribbon and trim the ends into
fishtails. Using a scalpel or craft
knife, cut two slots, one in either
side of the folder, just larger than
the width of your ribbon. Thread
the grosgrain through the slots,
and glue or tape down on the
inside of the folder.*

PENCIL POT

Constructed from five sections of card covered in Japanese paper, and held together with masking tape, this ribbon-trimmed pencil pot *(right)* is simple enough for children to make. Choose a thin, but hard-wearing, paper as a covering. Japanese paper is an attractive choice; the natural fibres interwoven into the paper give it an air of fragility, though in actual fact it is strong and sturdy.

To make the pot, first cut a piece of cardboard (A) approximately 12.5cm/5in square. Next, cut 4 rectangular pieces of cardboard (B), each measuring 13cm/5¼in by 11cm/4¼in. Lay out the pieces on a piece of Japanese or other strong paper (C) as shown, with the square piece in the centre and the rectangles overlapping it by approximately 1cm/½in. Cut four 11cm/4¼in strips of masking tape (D) and use to attach each

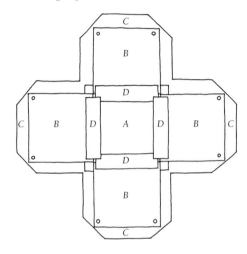

of the rectangles to the central piece – the tape will act as a hinge when you pull all the cardboard pieces into the pot shape.

Next, cut the Japanese paper to fit around the pieces, and, as if you are covering a book, fold the edges of the paper over and glue down onto the surface of each rectangle. Neatly mitre the paper to fit around the corners of the central square.

Using a hole punch, make two holes at the outer edges of each rectangular piece. Pull all the rectangular pieces towards the centre to form the basic pot shape, and secure the sides by threading four 40cm/16in lengths of 50mm/2in wide gingham ribbon through the holes and tying into bows.

PLEATED RIBBON
BLOTTER

*A handsome ribbon-edged
blotter will cover a not-so-
beautiful desk, as well as acting
as the focal point of your writing
table. Glue grosgrain ribbon
around the outer edges of the
blotter and trim each corner
with a Butterfly Pleat (see
p.116) made from 25cm/10in of
72mm/2³/4in wide grosgrain,
topped with the same length of
50mm/2in wide gingham
ribbon. This simple pleat has
myriad uses; try edging
cushions, bed linen, even
lampshades.*

   *If you tire of the existing
colour scheme, change the
colour of the blotting paper to
blue or burgundy and add eye-
catching ribbon corners to
match; or give the desk-top a
festive touch, and write your
Christmas cards on a blotter
decorated with corners of bright
red grosgrain surmounted by a
layer of tartan taffeta.*

FESTIVE FLAG CAKE

It is difficult to think of alternative cake decorations for children's birthdays when cars, teddies and Barbie dolls have already been exhausted. This fun flag cake, made with scraps of bright ribbon, is a festive riot of clashing colours.

For the sponge:

350 g/12 oz/1³/4 cups caster (superfine) sugar

350 g/12 oz/1¹/2 cups butter, softened

115 g/4 oz/1 cup ground almonds (finely ground blanched almonds)

2 tsp vanilla essence (extract)

¹/2 tsp almond essence (extract)

6 eggs (size 3), lightly beaten

170 g/6 oz/1¹/2 cups plain (all-purpose) flour

4 tsp milk

For the almond buttercream:

170 g/6 oz/³/4 cup butter, softened

170 g/6 oz/1¹/2 cups icing (confectioners') sugar

85 g/3 oz/³/4 cup ground almonds (finely ground blanched almonds)

1 tsp vanilla essence (extract)

1 tsp almond essence (extract)

To cover:

1.8 kg/4 lb ready-to-roll icing (fondant icing) (see Suppliers, p.123)

2 tbsp jam (jelly)

candy-coated chocolate sweets (candies)

Preheat oven to 180C/350F/gas 4. Line a 12.5cm/5in and 20cm/8in round cake tin (pan) with greaseproof paper.

Cream butter and sugar together. Beat in the ground almonds and essences (extracts) until light and fluffy. Add eggs a little at a time, beating after each addition. Sift flours together, then fold into creamed mixture and add the milk. Turn mixture into the tins (pans) and bake in the centre of the oven for 1 hour until well risen and golden brown. Turn out onto a wire rack and leave to cool.

Beat butter until light in colour. Add the icing (confectioners') sugar, ground almonds and essences (extracts) and beat until light and fluffy.

Trim top off each (cooled) cake, if uneven. Cut each cake in half and spread buttercream onto top of each cut layer (reserving about ¹/3). On a cake board, assemble the larger cake and coat the entire cake with a thin layer of buttercream. Roll out a sheet of ready-to-roll icing and cover top and sides of the cake, then rotate the palm of your hand on the top to smooth the icing and expel any trapped air. Puncture any air bubbles with a sterilized stainless steel knife. Smooth entire surface again. Place smaller cake on greaseproof paper and cover in the same way. Leave both cakes to dry for 24 hours. When dry, place smaller cake on top of larger one. Decorate with flags, candles, and sweets (candies) 'glued' on with dots of jam.

BELOW:

Using wire-edge ribbon will allow you to mould your 'flags' to flow and bend in the direction you want. Cut short lengths of ribbon. At one end, make neat fishtails. At the other end, attach a piece of double-sided adhesive tape. Place a cocktail stick on the outer edge of the tape and roll inwards.

TEA-TIME TREATS

FROM LEFT TO RIGHT:

*The minute buds of folded
ombré ribbon that adorn this
exquisite 'daisy-chain' look like
delicate sugar roses. Buy the
ribbon ready-made (see p.111),
or make your own by fashioning
tiny buds (see p.115), and
sewing onto thin green tape.*

*Low, flat cakes are easily
overloaded by too many frills
and flounces. Wind a sash of
pleated shot taffeta around the
cake and top with bright
pumpkin-orange ribbon.*

*Wire-edge ribbon can be
used to create wonderful foliage
and flowers (see p.115). This
decoration of folded ombré
ribbon (centre) looks just like a
freshly picked posy.*

*A wide, striped ribbon in
shocking fluorescents will make
the most of the humblest jam
tart or butterfly bun. Wrap
underneath the cake and finish
on top with an extravagant
Double Bow (see p.114).*

*A cake dressed with waves of
ruched ribbon (see p.115)
makes a wonderful centrepiece
for a celebration meal.*

27

CHILDREN'S TIDY-ALL

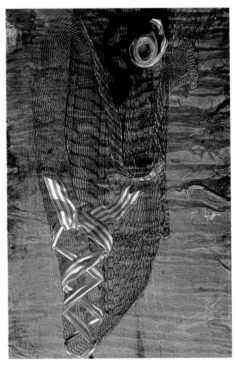

Children's rooms are their private havens, places where they can be untidy if they so choose, and where drawings, toys and books scattered all over the floor are a familiar sight. This beribboned tidy-all (*left*) might just persuade them to keep things more orderly. Constructed from wire netting, it has two separate compartments, secured at the sides with bows of brightly striped red and white wire-edge ribbon. Slotted behind the mesh, favourite pens and pencils, school books, comics and diaries are out of harm's way, but can still be easily spotted.

Don't worry too much about which type of ribbon to use. Ribbon is sturdier than you might think, and almost any woven ribbon will be strong enough to hold the sides of the netting in place. However, if you want to add decorative bows, you might prefer to use wire-edge ribbon, as it holds its shape well.

Wearing gloves to protect your hands from sharp edges, cut a single piece of wire netting to the desired size. Turn in all the raw edges and press them firmly to ensure no sharp wires are protruding. Turn the netting on its side and fold into the shape shown (*above right*) to form two 'compartments' – one at the top and one at the bottom. When you're happy with their size, secure one side of the lower compartment by threading a 1m/1¼yd

length of strong woven ribbon in a criss-cross pattern through the mesh. Tie the loose ends of the ribbon into a bow. Turn the netting over and repeat to secure the second side.

Now secure the sides of the upper compartment with two 1.5m/1¾yd lengths of ribbon. This time you will have *three* layers to thread the ribbons through: the front and back of the compartment, and the back of the tidy-all itself. Finish by tying the loose ribbon ends into bows.

The same tidy-all can easily be made in a smaller size. Thread with gingham or floral-print ribbon to make a storage rack for kitchen utensils.

YOU WILL NEED

- *Piece of wire netting measuring 1.5m/1¾yd by 0.5m/20 in*
- *5m/5½yd of woven ribbon*

NATURAL
WRAPPINGS

Wrapping a present is an art in itself, and beautiful wrappings can double the pleasure of the gift. Decorate parcels with natural materials such as berries, fir cones and leaves, and add ribbon trimmings to complement their textures and colours. Try sumptuous pleated velvets in earthy shades of brown and moss green, or bolduc in cream or pale beige.

Turn old cardboard boxes into gift boxes by covering with a layer of tissue paper and gluing on copper-, gold- or rust-coloured leaves. Paste another sheet of tissue paper over the top with PVA or white household glue (both are opaque, but dry clear). Allow to dry, then finish with a coat of varnish. Tie the boxes with festoons of leaves strung onto cotton tape.

Alternatively, dip raffia into tea to turn it burnished bronze, and use to bind your parcels. Or wrap gifts loosely in calico and secure with plaited strips of blue and cream bolduc ribbon.

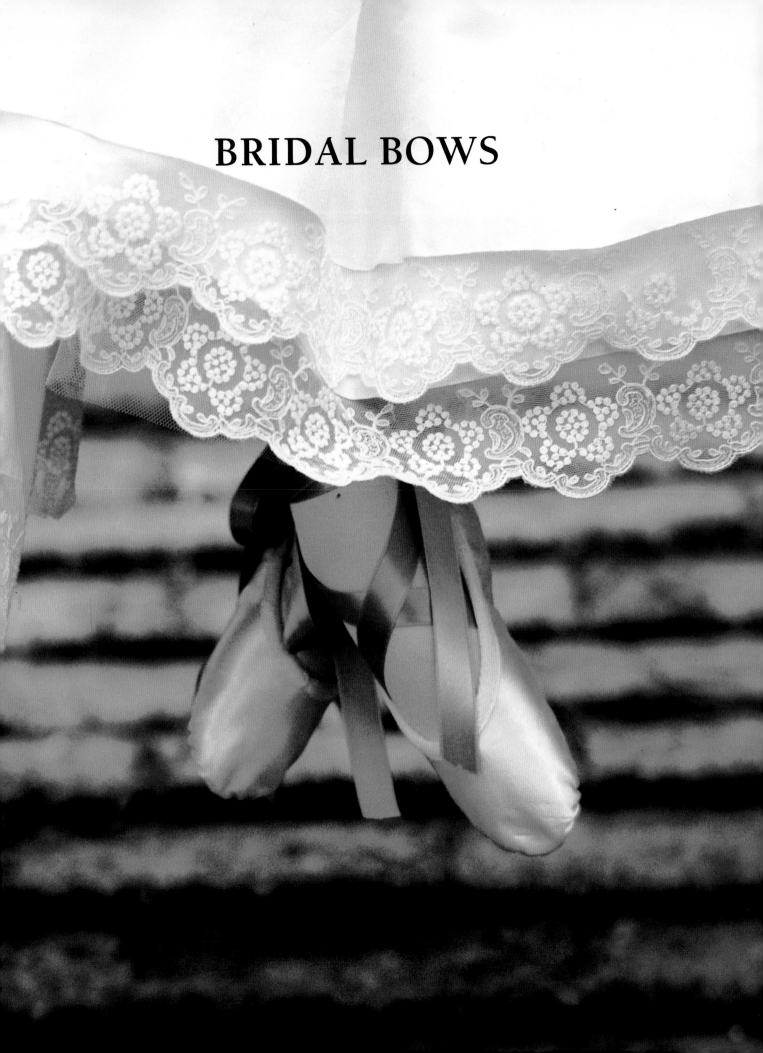

BRIDAL BOWS

BRIDAL BOWS

Shimmering ribbons teamed with flowers and foliage make eye-catching wedding decorations, whatever the season. For autumn nuptials, plunder the garden for berries, twigs and leaves, gather them into long garlands and tie on trails of delicate organdy ribbon. For summer weddings, festoon doorways and garden gates with exquisite full-blown pink roses tied with pink bows of every tone, to welcome your guests in. Be adventurous and mix ribbon textures in unexpected ways – try satin and the sheerest organdy with silver-edge metallic ribbon.

Preparing decorations for a wedding celebration can seem a daunting and unenviable task, but with judicious planning it can be exciting. Before you start, work out how much time and energy to devote to decorating each different location. There may be little point preparing elaborate table settings for the wedding meal, for instance, if it is going to be an informal buffet.

Start with the church. Give the interior little touches of elegance and colour in the form of ribbon and floral displays. The aim is to create a festive atmosphere, but bear in mind that weddings are sacred occasions, so your decorations must not overwhelm. Double Bows (see p.114) with long ribbon tails, and small

bunches of foliage used sparingly to frame the entrance to the church and deck the pew ends, will look subtle rather than showy. Two or three sizeable flower arrangements, strategically positioned, can look effective, especially if enhanced with lavish paper bows tied around the pedestals. Choose ribbons and blooms in colours such as white and yellow, that will hold their own in a huge dark church.

Next, concentrate on the journey from the church to the reception. Use swathes of white satin to create an eye-catching display of Twizzle-sticks (see pp.40-1) to line the churchyard path. Make up a selection of Rose Garlands (see pp.36-7) with burnt bronze and copper foliage – contrasting the rough texture of the leaves with the wispy featheriness of organdy bows – and drape around flower tubs or across tables. Multi-loop Bows (see p.116), made from layers of organdy backed with pink satin, will look stunning wherever they are set. Translucent organdy and shimmering satin complement each other beautifully and are wonderfully soft to the touch.

Finally, deck the reception hall or marquee with streamers of brightly coloured ribbon, and attach huge bows of cream or white paper twist to chair backs and tables.

PREVIOUS PAGES:
Don't overlook the smaller details: ribbons can transform little bridesmaids' shoes into slippers fit for a fairy-tale princess.

LEFT:
Even the most mischievous bridesmaids look angelic in white satin dresses and swathes of apricot, mauve and pale pink ribbon.

ROSE GARLAND

Whether they are teamed in simple bouquets or in more extravagant decorations such as this exquisite floral garland, ribbons and flowers make perfect partners. Complement the natural beauty of cream roses with delicate Multi-loop Bows, fashioned from layers of georgette and organdy ribbon; they are surprisingly quick and easy to make.

Using florists' wire, attach sprays of copper-beech leaves at appropriate intervals along the length of string (*see 1*). Leave a little space between each cluster. If they're packed in too tightly, they won't be able to flutter in the breeze.

Cut small strips of wire and push them through the top of the stems of the roses. Coil the wire down around the stems, leaving a little extra at the ends (*see 2*). Attach the roses at random between the sprays of beech leaves by twisting the loose wire around the string.

Cut 2m/2¹⁄4yd of the georgette and the same length of organdy. Start to make up a Multi-loop Bow, following step 1 of the method given on p.116. When the entire length of ribbon has been folded, gather it up and bind the centre with florists' wire (*see 3*).

To make the tail, cut 50cm/20in of each ribbon, lay the georgette on top of the organdy, and cut neat fishtails at both ends. Keeping the ribbons to-

gether, fold them in half and wire or sew onto the back of the bow. Pull out the loops of the bow to create flounces and attach to one end of the garland with florists' wire.

Make up a second Multi-loop Bow in exactly the same way, using the remaining ribbon. Attach to the opposite end of the garland, and pin the finished garland across your table or doorway.

YOU WILL NEED

- *Piece of string, approximately one and a half times as long as the surface you are decorating*
- *Florists' wire*
- *Beech leaves and cream roses, with at least 5cm/2in of stem left intact*
- *5m/5¹⁄2yd of 75mm/3in wide white organdy ribbon*
- *5m/5¹⁄2yd of 50cm/2¹⁄4in wide purple georgette ribbon*

RIGHT:

Bridesmaids with an eye-
catching display of Rose
Garlands (see previous pages)
and Twizzle-sticks (see
overleaf).

RIGHT:

Shimmering white satin ribbon tassels and iridescent beads glimmer in the sunlight.

ABOVE:

At the end of a long day, bridesmaids take a well-deserved break. With imagination, twizzle-sticks, uprooted from the flower-beds, become fairy wands.

TWIZZLE-STICKS

Twizzle-sticks swathed in the prettiest white satin and rose-pink organdy ribbons, and crowned with a circle of beads, make incredibly versatile wedding decorations. Use them to line the churchyard path and decorate the marquee, or simply stand them in the garden and let their shimmering satin tassels stream in the breeze.

First, using a hammer and thin nail, make a hole approximately 3cm/1¼in deep at the tip of the pole – this is the top of your twizzle-stick. Cut 3m/3¼yd of 25mm/1in wide white satin and attach one end to the top of the pole with clear adhesive tape. Wind the ribbon tightly along the length of the pole, until it is completely covered. Trim off any surplus ribbon and secure at the base with adhesive tape.

Roughly 25cm/10in from the top of the pole, hammer a small nail halfway in, leaving at least 5mm/³⁄₁₆in protruding (see 1). This will prevent the ribbon decorations from sliding down the pole.

Cut sixteen 30cm/12in lengths of 50mm/2in white satin. Cut neat fishtails in each ribbon at one end. To make the first tassel, take four of the ribbons and lay them on top of each other, stapling together at the uncut end. Repeat the process to make a further three tassels. Thread 25cm/10in of 3mm/1⁄8in wide white satin ribbon through the tassels, just underneath the staples, and tie in a double knot around the pole, just above the nail. Adjust the tassels so that they are evenly spaced around the pole.

Cut eight 16cm/6½in lengths of 50mm/2in wide white satin. Take two of the strips and fold over into loops. Place one loop on top of the other and staple the ends together. Repeat to make a further three double loops, then thread through a 25cm/10in strip of 3mm/1⁄8in wide white satin (see 2). Tie the collar of loops just above the tassels.

Cut three 1m/1¼yd lengths of white organdy and place to one side. Use the remaining white organdy, 25mm/1in wide white satin, and the pink organdy to make up a selection of Single or Double Bows (see p.114). Tie onto the pole above the collar of loops. Don't be too fastidious about neatness; mix and match bows of different sizes.

Thread brightly coloured beads onto a 20cm/8in length of florists' wire, leaving about 3cm/1¼in clear at either end. Loop the beaded wire into a circle and twist the ends together. Insert into the hole at the tip of the pole, securing with a little glue, if necessary.

Finish by tying the remaining 1m/1¼yd lengths of white organdy ribbon just beneath the ribbon tassels.

YOU WILL NEED

- *Wooden pole approximately 1m/1¼yd in length*
- *Hammer and small nails*
- *Clear adhesive tape*
- *6m/6½yd of 25mm/1in wide white satin ribbon*
- *6.5m/7yd of 50mm/2in wide white satin ribbon*
- *5m/5½yd of 25mm/1in wide white organdy ribbon*
- *3m/3¼yd of 25mm/1in wide pink organdy ribbon*
- *0.5m/20in of 3mm/1⁄8in wide white satin ribbon*
- *Heavy gauge florists' wire*
- *Pink beads*

BRIDESMAID'S RIBBON HOOP

This enchanting beribboned hoop is a novel variation on the traditional bridesmaid's posy, and, unlike a bunch of flowers, it won't wilt or droop after a few hours. For a delicate, feathery effect, tie satin or organdy ribbons in soft pastel shades into an abundance of bows, and attach to the hoop with narrow strips of pink satin. Finish with bunches of berries, sprigs of pale pink flowers and plenty of fresh green foliage.

Take a handful of long, thin pliable twigs and coil them into a circle. Bind the ends together with florists' wire. At three or four points around the circle, wind on some more wire – this will prevent the twigs from separating.

Next, make up a selection of Single Bows (*see p.114*) in varying pastel shades; try organdy in palest pink, and mauve speckled with silver. Bind the centre of the bows with long, narrow strips of pink satin ribbon.

Space the mauve bows around the hoop at regular intervals and tie on with the loose ends of the pink satin ribbon (*see 1*). Fill in the gaps with the pink organdy bows (*see 2*), secured in the same way. To finish, tie on small sprigs of pink flowers, with plenty of foliage still attached (*see 3*). To complete the picture, decorate the bridesmaid's slippers and hair to match.

For winter weddings, make up twig wreaths of winter foliage, and decorate with rosehips and berries, threaded onto coils of florists' wire. Finish with Christmas roses tied on with rich crimson velvet or tartan taffeta bows. Or for spring nuptials, adorn a twig hoop with the prettiest meadow flowers and sprigs of blossom, and finish with pale blue and primrose-yellow bows.

YOU WILL NEED

- *Pliable twigs, such as hazel, birch or clematis*
- *Florists' wire*
- *3m/3¹/4yd of 40mm/1¹/2in wide mauve organdy ribbon*
- *2m/2¹/4yd of 25mm/1in wide pale pink organdy ribbon*
- *2m/2¹/4yd of 3mm/¹/8in wide pale pink satin ribbon*
- *Flowers and foliage, to decorate*

HAIR BOWS & BRAIDS

Ribbons and bows can be used to create professional-looking hairstyles in minutes – guaranteed to appeal to young bridesmaids who are reluctant to sit still for hours while their tresses are primped and curled. This Victorian-style decoration of knots and bows has been achieved using pretty plum-coloured, satin-edge georgette ribbon; tie a wider version of the same ribbon around the bridesmaid's waist, fastening with a Single Bow *(see p.114)*. Dark, rich colours look all the more striking set against cream silk and lace – like blobs of damson jam in rice pudding. Alternatively, try a peaches-and-cream colour scheme, or a mixture of ribbons in peppermint, pale pink and white. Tie the ribbons into bows and attach to the hair, leaving the tails loose to float down the nape of the neck, like a glamorous hair extension.

Before you begin to dress the hair, brush it thoroughly to get rid of any tangles, then spray with water, to dampen it slightly. Part the hair in the centre, then divide into three sections; two at the front and one at the back. Plait the two front sections, securing the ends with hair bands *(see 1)*. Coil each plait into a knot at the side of the head, and secure in place with hair pins or grips.

Divide the section of hair at the back of the head into two: one section at the

nape of the neck, and one above it. Brush the uppermost section into a ponytail and keep in place with a hair band. Divide the ponytail into two and plait each section. Coil the first plait around the hair band and pin in place, then coil the second plait around the first and secure as before.

Take up the hair at the nape of the neck and plait *(see 2)*, coil into a knot and pin in place.

Make up four Single Bows from four 50cm/20in lengths of 23mm/⅞in wide plum georgette, binding the centre of the bows with a short length of the same ribbon, rather than sharp florists' wire. Keep the ribbon tails as long as possible, so that they can float at the nape of the neck *(see 5)*.

Finally, feed a hair pin through the back of each bow, by threading it through the ribbon binding the centre. Attach one bow to the top of each knot *(see 3 and 4)*, feeding the pin down through the hair.

Another simple idea for dressing a bridesmaid's hair is to adapt the Velvet Head-dress shown on p.50. Twist together narrow taffeta ribbons in pastel pink, mauve and cream; either finish the ends of the head-dress neatly, by tying them into bows, or leave them loose to stream in the breeze, like the ties on a Victorian bonnet.

4

5

Match the hair ribbons by wrapping a length of the same ribbon around the bridesmaid's waist and tying the ends into a loose bow.

CHRISTMAS
TRIMMINGS

CHRISTMAS TRIMMINGS

When time is running out and the turkey has still not been stuffed, you may feel that there's not a minute left for decorating, but ribbon decorations are so simple to make that they will make your Christmas preparations a pleasure rather than a chore. This chapter will provide you with plenty of inspiration, from impressive bows for gift wrapping or hanging swags of winter foliage, to beribboned tree decorations, wreaths and table settings.

Where decorations are concerned, Christmas is the one time of year when you can really go over the top. With the Christmas tree, fireplaces, tables, stair-cases and doors to be decorated, there is no surface that can't be decked with a few ribbon trimmings to create an instant festive atmosphere. And remember that at Christmas time, nothing that you choose to make will look out of place or incongruous. There are no rules to be governed by, and ribbon colours can range from sumptuous rich burgundies and purples, to glitzy gold and silver metallics, to natural jutes and cottons, teamed with raffia and berries.

Be as bold and daring as you like and build on your existing designs year by year, or ring the changes Christmas after Christmas, with your newest creations taking pride of place. This year, why not fix a huge elaborate Twisted Bow (*see p.122*) of shot taffeta to the top of the mirror; cover candles with criss-crossed strips of velvet (*see pp.50-1*); twist rich burgundy ribbons around the stems of candelabras or the hanging wires of chandeliers and lamps; or festoon the staircase with swathes of ivy interspersed with beautiful bows made from plum-coloured wire-edge ribbons. And don't overlook the smaller details: make up a selection of twig bundles to lay on the log basket next to the fire, and tie with velvet and grosgrain bows.

Prepare the Christmas table for your guests by tying napkins with purple and burgundy satin ribbons; the colours will look magical shimmering in the candle-light. Complete the look by tying bows around the stem of each wineglass and attaching lavish satin or velvet bows to chair backs.

If you're stuck for inventive gift ideas, adapt the candle-wrapping technique shown on pp.50-1 and make pretty stocking-fillers for the children by covering pencils in blue, green and orange ribbons. This technique is also useful for wrapping all those awk-wardly shaped gifts: decorating a plant pot with wide cotton tapes in sand, rust and red will set off a bright azalea or amaryllis beautifully.

PREVIOUS PAGES:
A twig wreath decorated with twists of gold wire mesh ribbon and delicate old man's beard looks striking on a cottage doorway, or above a mirror or mantelpiece. As a final touch, attach a trailing bow of shimmering gold wire-edge metallic ribbon.

LEFT:
Children always enhance the Christmas experience. Their excitement is infectious as they eagerly open presents and pull treats from the tree. Little bags of gold wire-edge woven ribbon, filled with sweets individually wrapped in ribbon scraps, should prove irresistible!

VELVET WRAPPINGS

ABOVE:

Both quick and easy to make, a head-dress of plaited velvet ribbons makes a wonderful Christmas stocking-filler.

Sumptuous velvet ribbons make ideal festive decorations. They come in a range of warm, rich tones that complement traditional Christmas arrangements of dark green winter foliage and red berries.

VELVET HEAD-DRESS

Christmas parties are an excuse for the whole family to dress up, and my daughters especially love to enter into the spirit of things and wear festive jewellery and hair decorations. Here (*left*), to make a change from a plain bow, my daughter Phoebe is wearing a head-dress of plaited ribbons in colours that match her dress. Make it by following the Plaited Ribbon Braid technique given on p.120, using narrow 7mm/¼in wide double-sided, pleated velvets in festive crimson and green. As the head-dress is a three-dimensional shape, both the front and back of the ribbons are visible, so choose ribbons with a good colour on the reverse side.

When you start to plait the head-dress it will be flat, but gradually, as you build layer upon layer, you will notice the ribbon beginning to change shape; pull the braid at both ends and it will magically transform into a concertina-like tube of ribbon. Twist the ends in opposite directions to achieve the spiralled effect shown here.

VELVET-WRAPPED CANDLES

These church candles (*below right*) encased in crimson and deep purplish-blue velvet would make a wonderful centrepiece for the Christmas table. Using non-drip candles will prevent the ribbon casing from becoming smeared with wax, but they should never be left unattended – don't allow them to burn down to ribbon level.

First, choose a thick, non-drip candle, and cut lengths of narrow velvet ribbon to approximately half its length. Turn the candle upside-down. Glue the ends of the ribbons to the base of the candle, keeping them close together and angling them slightly to accommodate the circular shape. Leave to dry.

Take approximately 2m/2¼yd of velvet in a contrasting colour, and pin this into the candle near the base – wherever you place the pin will be the back of your candle. Start to weave the ribbon through the hanging strips, under the first, over the second, and so on, gradually spiralling the ribbon around the candle. When you reach the end of the hanging strips, wrap a band of velvet around the loose ribbon ends, pinning at the back. Trim off any over-lapping ribbon ends. Finish by gluing a circle of velvet to the base of the candle.

LEFT:

Ribbon Wreaths (for method see p.120) make a refreshing change from traditional foliage-and-berry schemes. Hang larger ones on the door and smaller ones on the tree, or place them around the base of ribbon-wrapped candles (see below). Experiment with varying ribbon widths to achieve different patterns, or weave in gold cord or strings of purple beads.

SPARKLING
METALLICS

ABOVE & ABOVE RIGHT:
*Ribbons trimmed with silver and
gold look their sparkling best in
candle-light. Wrap ribbon
patterned with swirls of metallic
glitter around the struts of
chandeliers or candelabras.*

BELOW RIGHT:
*Simple wreaths of wired
chestnuts and onions make
wonderful year-round
decorations for the kitchen
window. At Christmas time,
customize them with a few
bows of opulent silver- or
gold-edged ribbon.*

52

FESTIVE FLOWERS

ABOVE & ABOVE LEFT:
*For vibrant Christmas colour, fill
the house with berries, foliage and
fresh flowers, and tie with bright
ribbons. Here, loops of indigo
wire-edge ribbon and narrow
strips of violet satin mirror the
vivid hues of winter anemones.*

LEFT:
*Even the smallest gift, such as a
box of chocolates, can be beautifully presented. Cover the box
with shiny gold paper, and tie with
sumptuous gold-edged taffeta. For
the prettiest of finishing touches,
tuck two or three flower stems
through the loops of the bow.*

53

A BEVY OF BOWS

Experiment with a range of different bows for decorating the tree, hanging swags and garlands, or stylish gift wrapping.

BELOW:

A broad wire-edge red ribbon, patterned with gold, has been fashioned into a Single Bow (see p.114). Add a second, trailing ribbon tail to make a real impact.

FAR LEFT:

A huge Double Bow (see p.114)
of wire-edge paper ribbon takes
minutes to make. Use at least
3m/3^{1}/4yd of ribbon and fan out
the loops and tails of the bow.

LEFT:

A cut-edge ribbon with an
overlocked, gilt wire edge looks
magnificent wrapped into a
lavish Twisted Bow (see p.122).

BELOW:

An elegant Wrap-over Bow (see
p.123) of grosgrain topped with
sumptuous purple velvet.

INTERIOR
MAGIC

INTERIOR MAGIC

If the ribbon decorations in your home extend only so far as a single bow on a lampshade or above a picture frame, you will probably be wondering how ribbons can be used to transform an interior. This chapter is packed with simple projects for ribbon furnishings and trimmings that can be adapted to suit any home, whether grand country mansion, cosy cottage or sophisticated city apartment. All you have to do is select the right ribbon for your needs. Delicate silks and jacquards are ideal for creating a pretty, old-fashioned look (see our antique-style bed linen on pp.68-71), but for a contemporary feel, go for bright colours and unusual textures, such as the vivid pink, plum and orange grosgrain ribbons used to create the eye-catching Woven Screen on pp.72-5.

If you're uncertain where to begin, start with the simplest technique of all – the bow. Tiny Single or Double Bows (see p.114), used to trim lamps, curtains, cushions and picture frames, can transform an interior at minimum expense. Try more elaborate effects, such as Twisted or Wrap-over Bows (see pp.122-3), for adorning curtains and dressing tables.

Cutting and gluing techniques are equally effective, and can be great time-savers. Frame pictures or photographs with gold foil-printed paper ribbon; just cut the ribbon into the appropriate lengths and glue down around the picture. A more ambitious scheme is to create a unique panelled room by gluing red and green shot moiré grosgrain around doorways, or gluing one or two ribbon stripes along a wall to create a picture rail.

Soft furnishings are more traditional subjects for ribbon decoration, but don't be daunted if your needlework skills are a little rusty. Projects such as the ribbon curtains on pp.64-7 take only minutes to make. Tie streamers of green and blue cotton tape onto a garden cane, decorate the ribbon ends with shells (see pp.66-7) and string across the doorway to a beach hut; or adapt the basic idea, and team blue and white gingham ribbons with plain white tape to make a pretty striped curtain for the nursery window.

Ribbons offer an easy way to co-ordinate the whole interior. Why not give a plain sofa Regency-style stripes by covering it with wide jacquard ribbons? Use the same jacquard to make bows to wrap around cushions. Attach bows to chair backs – paper twist is easy to manipulate and creates a stylish look for dinner parties – or lay stripes of wide satin over the seat, weighting the ends with ribbon tassels (see left).

PREVIOUS PAGES:

The key to creating a homely atmosphere lies in the tiniest of details. Decorate a bare shelf or mantelpiece with fragrant flowers and lavender bags of shot organdy, tied with pink and lilac satin ribbons.

LEFT:

Tasselled Turks-head Knots (see pp.80 and 121) make wonderful embellishments for bedspreads, table cloths and curtain tie-backs. Try tassels in eye-catching fluorescent shades, or, for understated elegance, plump for ombré ribbon, with colours shading from dark grey through to white.

FOUR SIMPLE TIE-BACKS

LAYERED BOW TIE-BACK

Take 2.7m/3yd each of 100mm/4in wide black grosgrain, 75mm/3in wide cream grosgrain and 50mm/2in wide black picot-edge grosgrain ribbon.

Cut 1.5m/1¾yd of each ribbon. Place the black grosgrain on a flat surface and lay the cream grosgrain on top, positioning it directly in the centre of the black ribbon. Pin in place. Next, lay the black picot-edge ribbon on top of the cream ribbon. Stitch all three ribbons together by machine-sewing along the length of the black picot at either side, 5mm/³⁄₁₆in from each outside edge.

Make points at either end of the layered ribbon by folding the ends over diagonally and sewing in place.

Cut 20cm/8in of each ribbon and sew together as before. Place to one side.

Make the larger layered ribbon into a Single Bow with a long ribbon tail (*see p.114*). Wrap the 20cm/8in layered ribbon around the middle of the bow and sew the loose ends together.

To make the tie-back itself, sew the remaining 1m/1¼yd ribbons together and make points at the ends as before. Stitch the layered bow onto the tie-back, then sew a small metal ring to each pointed end. Loop the tie-back around the drawn curtain, attaching the rings to hooks on the window frame.

FRAYED RIBBON TIE-BACK

Take 3.3m/3¾yd of 50mm/2in wide ombré ribbon and cut off the neat woven or wire edges along both sides. Gently tease out the threads to make a fringe roughly 7mm/¼in deep at either side.

Cut a piece of black fabric 67cm/26½in by 14cm/5½in and a piece of lightweight interfacing the same length but 11cm/4¼in wide. Place the interfacing on top of the fabric, and fold the lengthways edges of the fabric over to enclose the interfacing. Tack down. Cut a second piece of fabric the same size as the first, fold over 15mm/⅝in of fabric along top and bottom, and tack down.

Place the first fabric piece interface-up, then lay two lengths of fringed ribbon along the top and bottom so that they overlap it by about 2cm/¾in. Top with the second piece of black fabric, then sew all the layers together. Sew the two ends of the layered piece together, then form into a bow by binding the centre with a length of black fabric.

For the tail, cut two more pieces of black fabric 57cm/22½in by 14cm/5½in and sew together with frayed ribbon in between as for the bow, but omitting the interfacing and turning under the ends. Slip the tail through the band binding the centre of the bow. Trim the tail with gathered, fringed ribbon.

YOU WILL NEED:

- *Dressmakers' pattern paper*
- *1.5m/1³/₄yd of 90cm/36in wide cream silk fabric*
- *50cm/20in of 90cm/36in wide lightweight interfacing*
- *One spool each of black and cream sewing cotton*
- *4m/4¹/₂yd of 15mm/⁵/₈in wide black grosgrain ribbon*
- *4m/4¹/₂yd of 25mm/1in wide black wire-edge ribbon*
- *Assortment of black and clear glass beads*
- *Black buttonhole thread for stringing beads*
- *Two 2cm/³/₄in metal rings*

NOTE: *Each square on grid measures 10cm/4in by 10cm/4in*

BEADED TIE-BACK

Following the diagrams below, make two patterns from dressmakers' paper – one for the frill and one for the tie-back shape – and cut out.

Pin the frill pattern piece to the cream silk fabric, placing it lengthways parallel to the selvedge, and leaving enough room for a 1.5cm/⁵/₈in seam allowance. Cut out the frill shape, cutting 1.5cm/⁵/₈in from the edge of the pattern piece to allow for the seam. Now cut a second frill in the same way.

Allowing for a 1.5cm/⁵/₈in seam allowance, cut two tie-back pieces from the cream silk. To fit these two pieces onto the remaining silk, position the first

lengthways as for the frill and the second widthways across the fabric.

Cut a piece of interfacing the same size as the two silk tie-back pieces. Place the two silk tie-back pieces together with right sides facing. Then place the interfacing on top of the two silk pieces. Pin these three layers together along the side and jagged edges.

Leaving the curved top edge open, machine stitch the tie-back 1.5cm/⁵/₈in from the edge along the sides and the jagged lower edge, removing the pins as you stitch. Trim the interfacing close to the seam. Trim the seam to about 7mm/¹/₄in and clip off the seam allowance across the points of the jagged edge. Clip across the seam allowance at intervals along the side edges to ease the curves. Turn right side out and press.

Omitting the interfacing, sew the two frill pieces together in the same way, again leaving the top edge open. Turn the stitched frill right side out and press.

Pin black grosgrain ribbon to the right side of the frill along the bottom (jagged) edge, lining the lower edge of the ribbon up with the lower edge of the frill and turning under 7mm/¹/₄in of ribbon at the ends. Machine-stitch the ribbon in place along the centre.

Machine-stitch a line of long gathering stitches along the top of the frill

TIE-BACK PATTERN PIECE
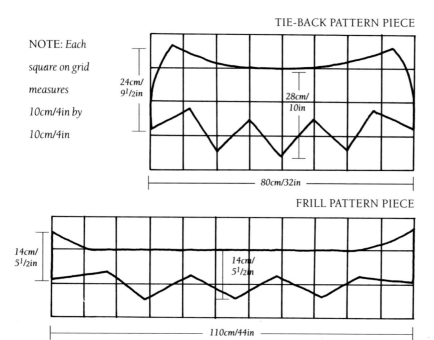
24cm/9¹/₂in · 28cm/10in · 80cm/32in

FRILL PATTERN PIECE
14cm/5¹/₂in · 14cm/5¹/₂in · 110cm/44in

7mm/¹/₄in from the raw edge. With the raw edges together, pin the wrong side of the frill to the right side of the tie-back, placing the sides of the frill 1.5cm/⁵/₈in from the sides of the tie-back. While pinning, ease the frill into place by pulling the line of gathering stitches and align the points of the jagged edge of the frill with those of the tie-back. Then stitch the frill to the tie-back just below the gathering stitches.

Cut two pieces of grosgrain ribbon 2cm/³/₄in longer than the length of the curved top edge of the tie-back. Lay the two ribbons on top of each other. Turning inside 1cm/¹/₂in at each end of both pieces, machine-stitch the two lengths of ribbon together lengthways as close as possible to one outside edge. Slip the raw top edge of the tie-back in between the two joined ribbons and pin, then machine-stitch in place.

Next, prepare the wire-edge ribbon by following steps 1-2 of the Ruched Flower technique given on page 115, but pulling the wire from both top and bottom corners of the ribbon to produce a gently ruched effect. Repeat the process at each corner of the ribbon to ruche a length long enough to fit along the sides and the lower jagged edge.

Pin the ruched ribbon to the side and lower edges of the right side of the tie-back, lining up the outside edge of the ribbon and the outer edge of the tie-back. Machine-stitch the ribbon in place along the centre. Tack the side points of the frill in place under the ruched trim.

Using the buttonhole thread, attach beads to the points of the jagged edges of the frill and the tie-back. When attaching the beads, first secure the thread to one of the points on the tie-back and string on the desired number of beads. Then, skipping the last bead, pass the threaded needle back up through the remaining beads and fasten off by securing it to the point once more.

To finish off, sew a metal ring to each of the two top corners of the tie-back for fitting to hooks on your window frame.

FLOWER ROSETTE

Following the method given on p.118, make up a Flower Rosette and attach to a curtain tie-back hook. The curtains can be swept back behind the hook to reveal the rosette. We used layers of gather-stitched black picot-edge, white and grey grosgrain, and decorated the centre of the rosette with white box-pleated grosgrain, rolled into a 'bud'. Alternatively, make up a Petal Rosette (*see p.119*) from wire-edge ombré taffeta ribbon, or a rosette with a combination of square and pointed petals.

RED GINGHAM CURTAIN

A scarlet gingham ribbon curtain provides a cooling shade from the sun's rays and frames the entrance to a summer house – the perfect hidey-hole where the Sunday papers can be read in peace. Even if your own garden retreat is more shed than summer house, a pretty rose-print or check ribbon curtain is a simple way to achieve country-style chic. All you need is enough strips of ribbon to go across the doorway and double over down to the floor. A broomstick or branch can take the place of a curtain pole. No elaborate hooks or fittings are required; simply knot the ribbons over the pole (*see below right*). A ribbon curtain made in this way is as easy to dismantle as it is to put together, so you can move it from room to room, or change the ribbons to suit your mood.

A doorway wreathed in ribbons is an inviting prospect, offering tantalizing glimpses of the room beyond. If you want the curtain to look just as stunning from the inside, choose ribbon patterned on both sides. Brighten a dingy hallway by framing the door that looks out onto the garden with a curtain of sheer organdy, in the palest shade of green, or autumnal rust and gold. The ribbons will look beautiful floating in the breeze with the sunlight streaming through them, and will enhance the view of the garden.

For a touch of Eastern exoticism, divide a room with swathes of wide organdy ribbons shot in orange and gold; sweep them to one side and hold in place with a bow of pleated, wire-edge ribbon. Or give a bedroom extra privacy by hanging a pole from the ceiling along one edge of a bed, and attaching cascades of silk georgette in rich purples to match a bedspread edged with velvet ribbon. This idea can be adapted for a child's room, with swathes of teddy bear print ribbon hanging over a baby's cot.

Ribbon curtains can just as easily be used to mask or veil. Unsightly coats and boots in a hallway can be hidden with strips of navy-and-white striped gros-grain, suspended from the ceiling. Hang an elegant double-face satin curtain between the dining-room and the kitchen to hide unsightly kitchen debris from dinner-party guests. You will be able to continue talking to your guests as you clear up the mess, without spoiling the atmosphere.

BELOW:

To attach your ribbons to the pole, first double over each length of ribbon. Thread the free ends of each loop over the pole, and feed them through the loop to pull up to a smart knot. Repeat this process until you have a full curtain across your portal or window.

SHELL CURTAIN

If you spent childhood summer holidays combing the beaches for beautiful shells which you have stored away, this hanging shell curtain will not take long to make. Dig out an assortment of shells – flat mussel shells washed by endless tides to a soft inky blue, exotic striped shells in coral pinks from faraway shores, pale conch shells – and make a tiny hole in each one, using a hand drill fitted with a 6mm/^{1}/4in drill-bit.

To hang your shells, choose cotton tape in colours that mirror the striped sand that you see in glass seaside ornaments – mustard, ochre, brown, plum and bleached white. Tie the free ends to a garden cane with a simple granny or fisherman's knot (see 1); don't neaten the edges, as a slightly dishevelled look will give your curtain a natural charm. Thread the ends of the ribbons through the holes in the shells and tie into a knot (see 2). String the curtain across the entrance to the beach hut, or drape it across the window, and as the sea breezes blow, the shells will make an enchanting sound.

You can easily adapt the curtain for a different location. Decorate the ribbon ends with stones, twigs, fir cones and any other natural treasures discovered on country walks and hang across a cottage window or doorway.

YOU WILL NEED

- *Assortment of shells*
- *Hand drill and 6mm/ ^{1}/4in bit*
- *10m/11yd of cotton tape in assorted colours*
- *Garden cane, broomstick or pole*

1

2

67

BERIBBONED BED LINEN

Ribbons in the prettiest floral hues – peony-and rose-pink, lilac and lavender – look wonderful against crisp white cotton. Choose luxurious silk and satin to give plain bed linen a sumptuously Victorian look, and trim the corners of pillows with simple bows or edge sheets with swirls of appliquéd ribbon. Weave ribbons through lace collars and button-holes to give night-dresses an extra feminine touch.

PYJAMA CASE

The ever-inventive Victorians decorated the lace edging of their cushions and other soft furnishings by threading narrow ribbons through the mesh – a simple technique that inspired the design of this easy-to-make pyjama case, interlaced with pink satin.

Following the diagrams (*see figs 2 & 3*) make a pattern from dressmakers' pat-tern paper and cut out the three shapes; one bag piece and two flap pieces. Lay out the pattern pieces on your cotton or linen, as shown (*see fig.1*), so that the straight grain of each flap piece is parallel to the selvedge. Cut out the bag piece, then the two flap pieces.

On the right side of one flap piece, mark out three pairs of slots for the ribbon to thread through, plus one odd one on each side (*see fig.4*).

Using the buttonholer on your sewing machine, and with matching thread, make buttonholes 5mm/^{3}/16in wider than the width of your ribbon on each slot mark. Cut open and press.

Join the long straight edge of the flap to the bag piece. Press the seam under the flap. Fold the bag in half, through the fold line (*see fig.3*), and with wrong sides inside. Press, then open out. Make a 5cm/2in hem on the other end of the bag and stitch down.

Using the piping (or zip) foot on your sewing machine, set the piping on the edge from the fold line up to and round the flap and down the second side to the fold line. Next, neaten the long straight edge of the second flap piece and lay on the stitched flap, right sides together. Pin and stitch (using the piping foot), keeping close to the piping.

Fold the bag through the fold line, with right sides together, and stitch along each side close to the piping, as before.

Turn the bag and flap right side out and press carefully. Cut the ribbon in half and attach one end of each piece to the underside of the front flap by stitching onto the seam that joins the flap to the bag. Slot each piece through the button-holes and tie the loose ends into a bow. Finally, slip-stitch the facing to the seam along the free edge.

YOU WILL NEED
- *Dressmakers' pattern paper*
- *Piece of firm cotton or linen 90cm/36in square, and matching sewing cotton*
- *2m/2^1/4yd of 15mm/^{5}/8in wide pink satin ribbon*
- *1.5m/1^3/4yd of pink piping*

CUTTING DIAGRAM

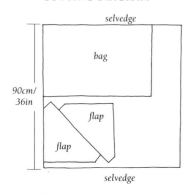

fig. 1

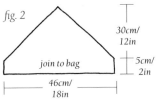

fig. 2

30cm/
12in

join to bag

5cm/
2in

46cm/
18in

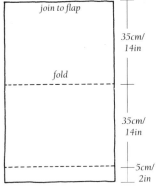

join to flap

35cm/
14in

fold

35cm/
14in

5cm/
2in

fig. 3

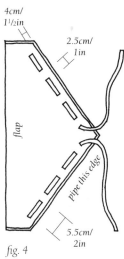

4cm/
1½in

2.5cm/
1in

flap

pipe this edge

5.5cm/
2in

fig. 4

69

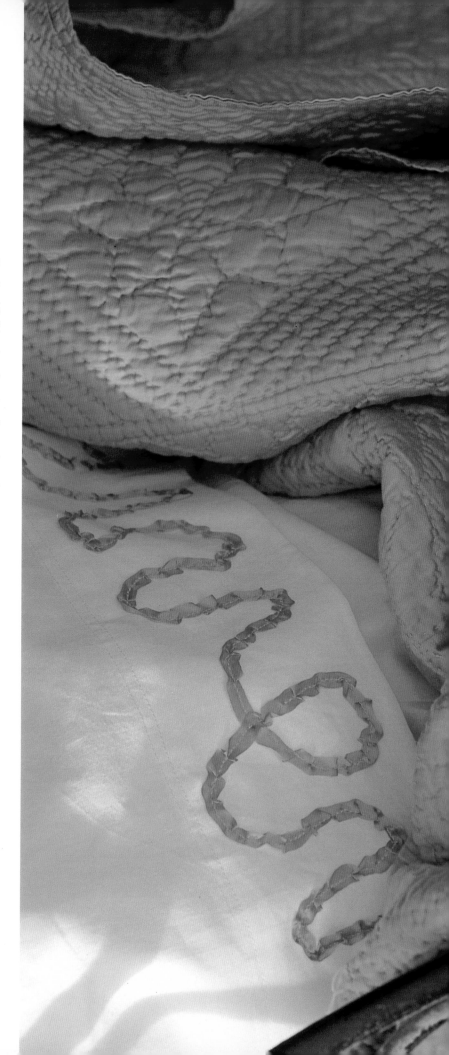

SILK RIBBON APPLIQUÉ

Appliquéd patterns of luxurious Chinese silk ribbon can turn plain sheets and pillowcases into beautifully co-ordinating sets of bed linen. Almost any type of woven-edge ribbon is suitable for appliqué, though to accommodate the curves of this flowing design *(right)*, we found that a narrow, 7mm/¼in wide silk ribbon was flexible and easy to handle.

Ribbon appliqué allows plenty of scope for imaginative designs. Try sewing on flower motifs made from tiny strips of ribbon, edging sheets with satin ribbon folded into peaks, or giving your bed linen a simple border of patterned ribbon, such as an exquisite jacquard with a design of delicate mauve, pink and blue roses *(see p.104)*.

Using dressmakers' chalk, lightly mark your chosen pattern onto the pillowcase or sheet. Estimate how much ribbon you will need by loosely pinning the ribbon onto the pattern (bear in mind that the ribbon will be slightly gathered, so allow a generous surplus).

Give the ribbon a slightly 'ruched' effect by gather-stitching along the centre with matching thread. Pin the gathered ribbon onto the pattern, then sew down the centre of the ribbon with matching thread, using running stitch and the occasional back stitch.

WOVEN SCREEN

This screen of woven grosgrain ribbons adds a burst of brilliant colour to a plain, white bathroom. Pick up the vivid plum, orange and pink scheme in tile or paint work, and decorate the room with coloured soaps to match.

Before you start, measure the width of the ribbon you are using, as this will determine the size of your frame. For this particular screen, we calculated the width of each panel to be 63.5cm/ 25in; this allowed for six vertical strips of 100mm/4in wide ribbon, with a 5mm/^{3}/$_{16}$in gap between each one.

To make the panels of your frame, lay out the pieces of wood to form three rectangles, with the shorter pieces of wood butting against the longer ones. Secure the joints with two or three staples. Drill holes roughly 6cm/2^1/$_4$in deep at the four corners of each panel, 2cm/^{3}/$_4$in in from each outside edge, then screw the pieces of wood together.

Next, divide the ribbons. Cut eighteen 2m/2^1/$_4$yd strips of plum grosgrain and place to one side. Divide the remaining plum ribbon into fifteen 90 cm/36in strips. Cut the orange ribbon into eighteen 90cm/36in strips and the pink into fifteen 90cm/36in strips.

Take the first panel and either lean it up against a wall, or lay it on the floor

YOU WILL NEED

- *Twelve pieces of softwood, each 4cm/1^1/$_2$in square; six 63.5cm/25in long, and six 1.6m/1^3/$_4$yd long*
- *Staple gun*
- *Drill and 6mm/^{1}/$_4$in bit*
- *Screwdriver and 35mm/ 1^1/$_2$in screws*
- *49.5m/54yd of 100mm/4in wide plum grosgrain ribbon*
- *16.2m/17^3/$_4$yd of 100mm/4in wide orange grosgrain ribbon*
- *13.5m/14^3/$_4$yd of 100mm/4in wide pink grosgrain ribbon*
- *Six hinges*

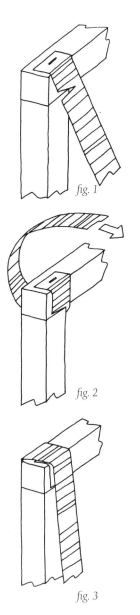

fig. 1

fig. 2

fig. 3

ABOVE:

The ribbons at the outer corners of each frame require cutting to fit snugly around the back and sides of the panel. Make a horizontal cut 4cm/1¹/2 in wide, then pull the ribbon around to the back of the frame, and up and over the top. Don't worry too much if your cuts aren't perfectly neat, as any messy handiwork will be hidden by the tightly woven ribbons.

– whichever you find easiest to work with. Take one of the 2m/2¹/4yd plum ribbons and, starting 5mm/³/16in in from the outer edge of the top left-hand corner of the panel, staple it to the top of the frame. About 4cm/1¹/2in down from the top of the ribbon, make a horizontal cut 4cm/1¹/2in wide (*see fig.1*), cutting from the left-hand side of the ribbon towards the centre. (This nick in the ribbon will ensure that it fits neatly around the back and sides of the panel, but don't worry if your hand is a little unsteady – the ribbon strips that cover the frame are interwoven very tightly and will hide any inexpert cutting.) Next, loop the ribbon round to the back of the frame, and flip it up and over the top (*see fig.2*). Pull it tight, and stretch it down to the bottom of the panel (*see fig.3*), keeping it taut. When you reach the bottom of the frame, take the ribbon underneath the base of the panel, and bring it back up around the back. Tuck the ribbon end over the flat surface of the frame and staple down.

Staple a second 2m/2¹/4yd plum ribbon to the top of the frame, leaving a 5mm/³/16in gap between it and the first ribbon. This time you can omit the cutting stage – simply loop the ribbon over the top of the panel, pull down to the base and secure at the back of the panel, as before. Attach a further three

2m/2¹/4yd ribbons in the same way, leaving a 5mm/³/16in gap between each one. Finally, attach the fifth and final ribbon (this will need to be nicked 4cm/1¹/2in from right to left before it is wound around the frame).

When all the vertical ribbons are attached, turn the panel over on its side. Take a strip of orange ribbon and align it up against what is now the outer edge of the right-hand corner of the frame. Staple to the frame, make a cut in the ribbon, as before, so that it fits neatly around the sides and back of the panel, and loop it around the top of the frame. Now begin a basic weave (*see p.117*), tucking the ribbon under the first plum ribbon, over the second, under the third and so on. Secure at the base as before. Next, weave in a strip of pink grosgrain, first taking it over the plum ribbon, then under, then over and so on, securing at the top and base as before. Follow with a strip of plum ribbon. Continue weaving with alternating strips of orange, pink and plum, finishing with a strip of orange (don't forget to nick this outside strip from left to right) until the panel is completely covered and there are no yawning gaps between the ribbons.

Make up the two remaining panels in exactly the same way then secure the three panels together with hinges.

FRILLS &
FURBELOWS

FRILLS & FURBELOWS

In the eighteenth and nineteenth centuries, ribbons were the ultimate fashion statement. Every item of clothing that could possibly be embellished was decorated with ribbon, and men's fashions were often more ornate that women's. The dandies of the day sported shoes decorated with ribbon rosettes, and trousers, doublets and shirts laced up with elaborate bows. Single ribbons were used as watch fobs, and even walking sticks were decorated with bunches of bright ribbon.

Today, if you ask people how they would wear ribbons, the replies are likely to be uninspiring. For most of us, the only idea that would spring to mind would be a bow in the hair. But there is a wealth of fabulous patterned, pleated and coloured ribbons just waiting to be exploited – all you need is a little imagination. The projects in this chapter use ribbons in unexpected, rather than traditional, ways. Why not surprise the man in your life, who would normally blanch at the very thought of wearing ribbons, with a pair of fun – and stylish – Dalmatian-spotted braces? Colour schemes can be as outrageous as you like – weave strips of deep-blue silk taffeta into a wrap, and edge with the brightest pink, lime-green and orange ribbons and Turks-head Knots (see pp.82-3).

Ribbon fashions can be either elegant or practical. Delicate ribbon textures are ideal for evening wear; weave red, gold and blue shot organdies into a stunning shawl to wear over your little black dress (see pp.80-1). To make a stylish bag and beach mat for a summer picnic (see pp.88-93), use hard-wearing grosgrains and knitted tape in sky-blue and gold.

You don't have to be a great seamstress or the next Coco Chanel to create fabulous beribboned outfits and accessories. Hats are some of the easiest items of clothing to embellish. You'll learn how to give a plain hat the *couture* treatment with a decoration of satin and wire mesh ribbons; or thread a wire-edge taffeta onto a hat-pin to lend a hat instant chic (see pp.94-7). Another interesting alternative is to cut a moon or star shape out of the crown of a felt or straw hat, and back the hole with a piece of patterned ribbon, glued to the inside of the hat. Or cut slits around the brim of your hat with a sharp scalpel (though do take care) and thread through a colourful ribbon.

Why not borrow a few techniques from other chapters ? Make ribbon roses (see p.115) and transform an old evening gown with a spray of pale pink satin buds. Or make up a Plaited Ribbon Braid (see p.120) in elegant black silk or velvet, and wear as a choker.

PREVIOUS PAGES:

Exquisite evening bags with Regency-style stripes of woven jacquard and embroidered ribbon.

LEFT:

Like the light streaming through a stained glass window, the delicate organdy ribbons that make up this beautiful shawl (see pp.80-1) glow gold, crimson and aquamarine.

ORGANDY SHAWL

This magnificent shawl of organdy ribbons, shot through with glowing sunset shades of gold and scarlet, makes a sensational fashion statement.

First, divide the 15m/16½yd of shot organdy into ten 1.5m/1¾yd strips, and the 16.2m/17¾yd of contrasting ribbon into eighteen 90cm/36in strips.

Cover the board with a sheet or canvas – this is your base. Lay out the first ten ribbons vertically on the board, keeping them close together so that they are just touching but not overlapping. Pin each ribbon at the top to secure in place.

Now start a basic weave, following the method given on p.117. Approximately

75mm/3in down from the top of the outermost ribbon, weave in the first 90cm/36in ribbon, feeding it over then under, over then under, and so on. Continue weaving until you reach the opposite side of the board, then pin the ribbon at both ends. You will probably find that there is about 75mm/3in of surplus ribbon at either side. Don't worry about these loose ends; they can be finished off neatly at a later stage.

Continue weaving until you have a full chequer-board of ribbons. At each point where the horizontal and vertical ribbons align, make a small tacking stitch with invisible thread. Remove the pins and neaten up the raw ribbon ends by cutting them into fishtails.

Use the four pieces of cord to make up four Turks-head Knots, following the method given on p.121. You should be left with a tight knot of cord, with a small hole in the top and a larger hole underneath. Take six of the 40cm/16in organdy ribbons and fold in half lengthways. Sew all the loose ends together tightly. Tie a piece of cord around the top of the 'tassel', then thread it upwards through the hole in the base of one of the Turks-head Knots, pulling the tassel up with it so that the sewn end is hidden in the middle of the knot. Tie one knot to each corner of the shawl.

YOU WILL NEED

- *Piece of softboard measuring 1.75m/2yd by 1m/1¼yd*
- *15m/16½yd of 75mm/3in wide shot organdy ribbon*
- *16.2m/17¾yd of 75mm/3in wide shot organdy ribbon in a contrasting colour*
- *Twenty-four 40cm/16in lengths of 38mm/1½in wide shot organdy ribbon in assorted colours, for the tassels*
- *Four 1.5m/1¾yd lengths of cord in contrasting shades for the Turks-head Knots, plus a little extra for tying the tassels to the shawl*

SILK TAFFETA WRAP

YOU WILL NEED

- *Piece of softboard measuring 1.75m/2yd by 1m/1¼yd*
- *14.4m/15¾yd of 100mm/ 4in wide shot silk taffeta ribbon*
- *14.4m/15¾yd of 100mm/ 4in wide shot silk taffeta ribbon in a contrasting colour*
- *Four 1.6m/1¾yd lengths and four 90cm/36in lengths of brightly coloured shot silk taffeta ribbon, for edging*
- *Four brightly coloured tasselled Turk's-head Knots (see p.80)*
- *Gold- or silver-coloured beads*

This iridescent beaded wrap of deep sea-blue silk taffeta, shot in sapphire and rich purplish-brown, catches the light and will attract the eye of every passer-by. It's a perfect example of how changing a ribbon type or colour can alter the whole appearance of a project. The basic making-up method given below is almost identical to that used for the Organdy Shawl on pp.80-1, but using sumptuous shot taffeta gives a dramatically different result.

Cut nine 1.6m/1¾yd lengths of shot taffeta, and sixteen 90cm/36in lengths of taffeta in a contrasting colour. Lay out the first nine strips vertically on your piece of softboard, keeping them close together

so that they are just touching, but not overlapping. Secure the ribbons at the top with pins.

Now start to weave through the horizontal ribbons, following the method given on p.117, until your basic wrap is complete. At each point that the horizontal and vertical ribbons intersect, make a small tacking stitch. The ends of your ribbons should be protruding by about 1cm/½in – this is your seam. Take out the pins and tack carefully along the seam edges, keeping close to the last straight ribbon edge, then machine-sew over your tacking stitches.

Lay out the first edging strip along one side of the wrap, so that it just covers the loose ends of the ribbons and lines up neatly against the last straight ribbon edge. Hand-stitch the edging strip to the wrap, sewing up through the existing machine stitches. Turn the wrap over, and repeat the process on the other side. Continue until you have edged the entire wrap. To give a neat finish, the raw ends of the ribbon weave can be rolled up inside the edging strips, tucked under and tacked in place. Either leave your edging strips loose or sew together. Sew tiny beads at each point in the wrap that the ribbons intersect, to cover your tacking stitches, and attach a tasselled Turks-head Knot to each corner.

SPOTTED BRACES

Braces are practical, but can be fun, too. Whether you favour black or white spots, bold stripes or vivid colours, the possibilities for creating your own designs are endless. Festive occasions offer the perfect excuse to experiment with the most eye-catching of ribbons; a pair of braces fashioned from red tartan ribbon, for instance, would make a wonderful Christmas gift. The braces fittings are easy to get hold of – try your local haberdashers' or department store.

Thread the top of your sewing machine with white sewing cotton and wind black sewing cotton onto the bobbin. Lay the length of mock suede on top of the black grosgrain ribbon with the wrong sides together (*see fig. 1*). With the mock suede facing upwards, machine-stitch close to the edge down one side of the two layers of ribbon. Then sew down the other side in the same way.

Cut the joined strips into three sections: two 1m/1¼yd long and one 40cm/16in long (*see fig.2 overleaf*).

Next, cut three 9cm/3½in lengths of 30mm/1¼in wide black elastic. Feed one end of an elastic strip through one of the rings and the other end through a trouser clasp. Fold under 2cm/³⁄₄in of one end of the elastic and lay it over the other end. Then join the elastic where it overlaps by machine-stitching it to-

YOU WILL NEED

- *One spool each of black and white sewing cotton*
- *2.5m/2³⁄₄yd of 38mm/1¹⁄₂in wide zebra- or Dalmatian-print mock suede ribbon*
- *2.5m/2³⁄₄yd of 38mm/1¹⁄₂in wide black grosgrain ribbon*
- *30cm/12in of 30mm/1¹⁄₄in wide strong black elastic*
- *Braces fittings: 3 rings, 3 trouser clasps and 2 lever clips*
- *Piece of black leather measuring 11cm/4¹⁄₂in by 8cm/3¹⁄₂in*

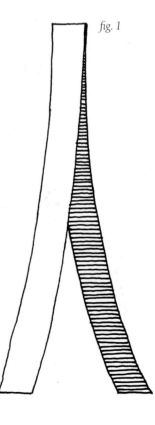

fig. 1

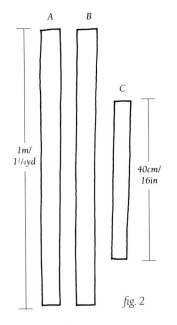

fig. 2

gether close to the clasp *(see fig.3)* using matching sewing cotton. Join each of the other two strips of elastic to a clasp and ring in the same way.

Feed the shorter braces' strap (C) through the ring on one of the finished elastic clasp-fittings (D) *(see fig.4)*. Fold the strap in half widthways with the wrong sides together. Tack the ends of the strap together and set aside.

Feed one of the longer straps through a lever clip (E) with the right side of the clip on the right side of the strap *(see fig.5)*.

Now feed the same strap through the ring on an elastic clasp-fitting and take the end of the strap back up to the lever clip, feeding it through the ring opening at the back of the clip. With 3.5cm/1¼in of the strap end pulled through the back of the clip, fold under 1.5cm/⅝in of the end. Tack the end to the wrong side of the strap, then machine-stitch in place *(see*

fig.6) using white sewing cotton. Attach the remaining lever clip and elastic clasp-fitting to the other long strap.

On a flat surface, arrange the three straps patterned side up and over-lapping to form a Y-shape *(see fig.7)*. Position the longer straps (A and B) at about a 45 degree angle to each other. Pin the straps (A, B and C) together. If necessary, adjust the lengths of the longer straps, then tack the three straps together where they overlap.

Cut two pieces of leather (F) into the tapered shape shown below *(see fig.8)*. Place one piece of leather on the wrong side of the strap join and one on the right side. To complete the braces, machine-stitch the leather pieces together all along the outside using matching sewing cotton *(see figs 9 & 10)*. This join will take a lot of strain so make sure your stitches are secure.

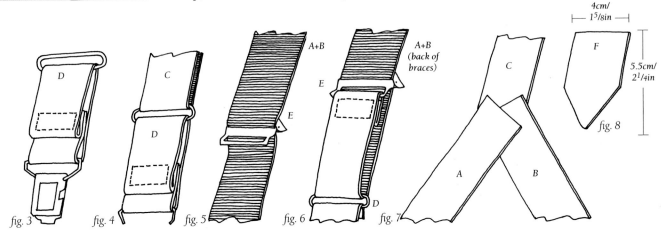

fig. 3 *fig. 4* *fig. 5* *fig. 6* *fig. 7* *fig. 8*

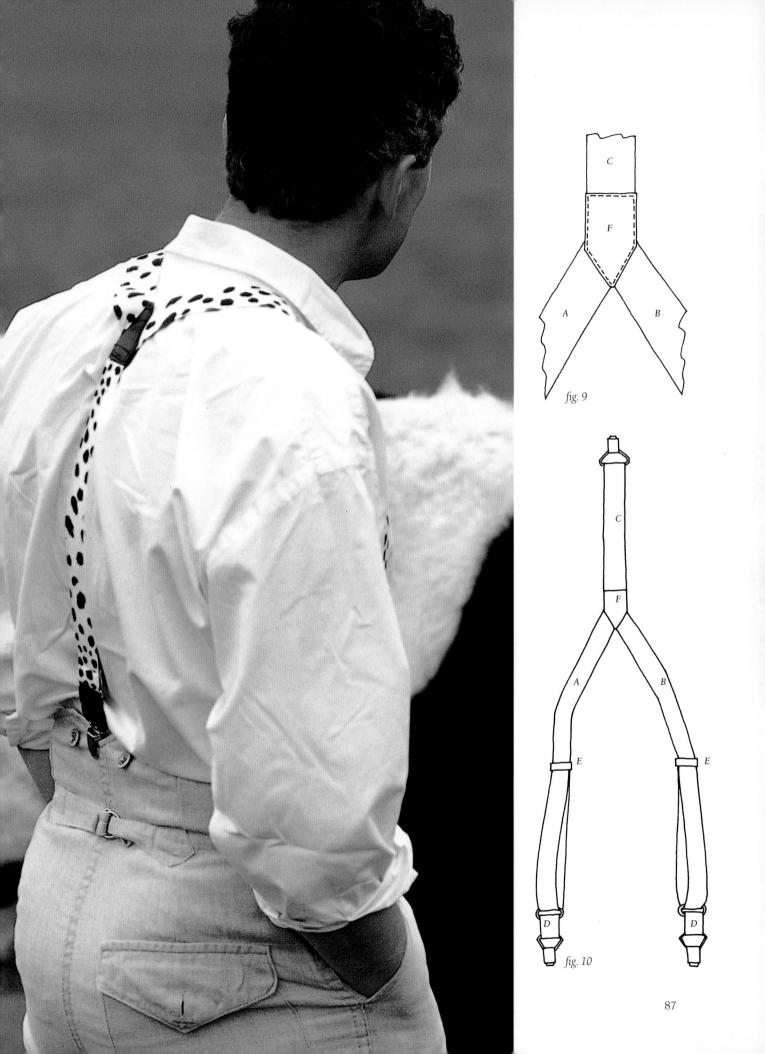

fig. 9

fig. 10

A DAY AT THE BEACH

*Make a whirligig to stake out
your spot by attaching several
3m/3^1/4yd lengths of red, green,
blue, pink and yellow satin to a
wire ring suspended from the top
of a ribbon-covered pole. Check
which way the breeze is blowing
to prevent the whirligig blowing
into the picnic, then stand it
securely in the sand.*

YOU WILL NEED

• *43.5 /47^1/2yd of 38mm/
  1^1/2in wide light blue
  grosgrain ribbon*
• *1.2m/1^1/4yd of 90cm/36in
  wide iron-on interfacing*
• *Masking tape*
• *1.6m/1^3/4yd of 90cm/36in
  wide fabric for lining, and
  matching sewing cotton*
• *One spool each of light blue
  and gold sewing cotton*
• *3m/3^1/2yd of 38mm/1^1/2in
  wide gold grosgrain ribbon*
• *Two 77cm/30in lengths of
  thick strong cord, for core of
  straps*
• *Piece of strong cardboard
  measuring 49cm/19^1/2in by
  23cm/9in, for base of bag*

A day out at the beach means packing
buckets, spades, suntan lotion, towels,
and a huge picnic. With so many things
to carry, this hard-wearing, washable
grosgrain bag *(right)* will be invaluable.

You'll also need somthing to sit on. Why
not create a beach mat *(see overleaf)* from
hard-wearing canvas, topped with a
baby-soft blanket, and edged with
military knitted tape in stripes of gold,
electric- and powder-blue.

WOVEN BEACH BAG

Cut a piece of paper 72cm/28^1/2in wide
by 99cm/39in long. This is your paper
template *(see fig.1 overleaf)* for the finished bag size. Next, cut nineteen
110cm/43in lengths and twenty-six
80cm/32in lengths of light blue ribbon.

Lay the paper template on a flat table
or a large board. Then lay the nineteen
longer strips of ribbon side by side
lengthways on top of the template so that
they extend an equal distance past the
template at each end. The ribbons should
just cover the width of the template and
should be just touching each other, but
not overlapping. Secure one end of the
ribbons ends in place with a long strip of
masking tape positioned 2.5cm/1in from
the edge of the template.

Follow the basic weaving technique
given on page 117, interweaving the

twenty-six shorter horizontal strips over
and under the secured vertical strips.
Continue until you have what looks like
a continuous rectangle of material, with
no visible gaps between the ribbons.
These horizontal strips should just cover
the length of the template, but extend an
equal distance past the template at each
side. Now secure the three remaining
sides with masking tape 2.5cm/1in from
the edges of the template.

Next, cut a piece of iron-on interfacing 75cm/30in wide by 102cm/40in
long. Cut a piece from the lining fabric to
the same size and set aside.

Lay the interfacing over the ribbon
weave, positioning it so that a 1.5cm/
^{5}/8in seam allowance all around the
interfacing extends beyond the last
straight edge of ribbon on all four sides.
Tack the interfacing in place just inside
the outside edge.

Using a hot iron, press the interfacing
in place so that it sticks firmly. Don't let
the iron touch the masking tape.

Turn the ribbon weave over so that the
right side is facing upwards. Then fold
the ribbon weave in half widthways with
the right sides together and pin the sides.
Machine-stitch the sides of the bag
together just outside the last straight
ribbons, leaving the top open. Trim off
the ribbon ends along the seams so that

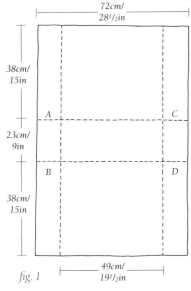

fig. 1

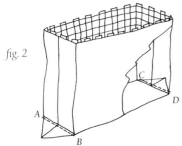

fig. 2

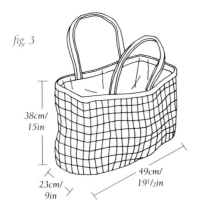

fig. 3

they are flush with the edge of the interfacing and press the seams open.

Keeping the bag wrong side out, fold into a three-dimensional shape as shown (*see fig.2*). Machine-stitch across the point at the corners on one side, from A to B. Do the same from C to D on the other side. Trim the weave to 1.5cm/⅝in from the seams. Turn right side out.

Tack along the open top edge of the bag 1cm/½in inside the outside edge of the last straight ribbon. Trim the weave close to the edge of this ribbon.

Machine-stitch the lining fabric together in the same way as the bag, making 1.5cm/⅝in wide seams. Trim 1.5cm/⅝in off the open top rim.

Keeping the lining wrong side out, insert it inside the ribbon-weave bag. Pin the top rims of the bag and the lining together, aligning the raw edges and side seams. Tack in place and remove pins.

Fold a 1.5m/1¾yd length of gold ribbon in half lengthways and press. Place the creased ribbon over the top rim of the bag and tack in place, folding under the end where it overlaps the beginning of the ribbon. Machine-stitch the gold ribbon in place.

Cut two pieces of lining fabric measuring 52cm/20¾in by 26cm/10¼in. With right sides facing, machine-stitch together along three sides, 7mm/¼in from the edge, leaving one short side open. Insert the piece of cardboard, turn the raw ends to the inside and hand-stitch together. Insert inside the bag.

Cut two pieces of gold and two pieces of light blue grosgrain ribbon 5cm/2in longer than the desired strap length. Lay a gold strip of ribbon on top of a blue strip with the wrong sides together. Machine-stitch the ribbons together lengthways 7mm/¼in from one edge.

Insert one piece of cord between the joined ribbons and machine-stitch the other side of the ribbons together lengthways. Make a second strap in the same way. Folding under the ends, sew neatly to the inside of the bag (*see fig.3*).

RIGHT & FAR RIGHT:

BEACH MAT

This beach mat is edged with stripes of 67mm/2½in wide military knitted tape. To create neat, mitred corners, lay one length of tape on top of the other. 67mm/2½in down from one outside edge, sew diagonally across to opposite corner. Pull top ribbon over to one side.

TOP HATS

For most of us, hats are accessories that languish at the back of the wardrobe for months at a time until they are hauled out and dusted down for a special event such as a wedding or christening. We wear them so rarely that buying a new hat every season just isn't a viable option, but there's no reason why we shouldn't update the same hat for each occasion by adding a few new ribbon trimmings.

By far the easiest way to give a plain hat a sophisticated finish is to trim the front or the back with a lavish satin bow. But why not experiment with an unusual combination of satin and wire mesh ribbon (*see 4 and 6 overleaf*)? Even simpler, why not make a fabulous hat-pin threaded with wire-edge ribbon (*see 2 and 3 overleaf*)? It can be made in minutes, without the need for a single stitch. I used a hat-pin decorated with a ball of cord, though if you can't find anything similar, you can make your own by gluing black cord around a wooden bead, then pushing an ordinary hat-pin through it. Finish by sewing a black tassel onto the cord of the ball.

For ultimate chic, keep hat decorations simple. Add a few roses made from folded wire-edge ribbon (*see p.115*), or tie two Turks-head Knots (*see p.121*) to the brim. There is no secret to attaching ribbon trimmings: just tack-stitch them onto the hat, using a strong thread, such as buttonhole thread. Start with a good knot, and work from the inside of the hat through to the outside, finishing off tightly on the inner hat band.

LAYERED SATIN BOW

First, cut 60cm/24in of 100mm/4in wide double-face cream satin ribbon and sew the loose ends together to form a circle. Repeat with a 50cm/20in and 40cm/16in length of the same ribbon. Flatten the largest circle into a loop, and lay it out so that the stitched join is at the back of the loop. Lay the 50cm/20in and the 40cm/16in loops directly on top. Pinch all three loops in the centre and gather-stitch them together across the middle. Bind a narrow strip of satin around the centre, hiding the stitches.

Wind a piece of 100mm/4in wide cream satin around the crown of your hat. Sew the loose ends together either at the side or the front of the hat – wherever you want the finished bow to go. Next, make the 'tail' of the bow. Cut 25cm/10in of the same ribbon and fold in half lengthways. Gather-stitch the loose ends together. Sew the tail to the hat by stitching the gathered end to the top of the satin band, covering your earlier stitches. Finally, place the looped bow over the top of the tail and stitch in place.

LEFT:

An elaborate bow of layered satin ribbon looks complicated to make, but in actual fact is formed in easy stages. For a very different look, trim the hat with a Twisted Bow (see p.122) of crimson taffeta.

95

1 2
4 5

3
6

WIRE MESH BOW

Cut enough 100mm/4in wide black satin ribbon to wrap once around the crown of your hat. Attach with a few small tacking stitches made close to the base and top of the ribbon. Now cut a piece of 170mm/7in wide black wire mesh long enough to wrap around the crown of the hat, allowing a little extra for moulding into shape. Wrap loosely around the satin band and tack the loose ends together. Secure the mesh with a few tacking stitches close to the hat brim or just above the satin band. Gently pull the wire mesh away from the top of the hat crown, so that it fans out slightly.

Cut another piece of the same wire mesh ribbon and form into a large Single Bow (*see p.114*). Pinch the centre of the bow and wind a short length of satin around it. Stitch the finished bow onto the wire mesh band, and, to secure the bow in place and stop it from wobbling, catch-stitch the top and base of each loop to the hat brim and crown.

RUCHED RIBBON HAT-PIN

Cut a long piece of black wire-edge taffeta ribbon and thread it onto a hat-pin, bunching it up tightly. Now gently pull and tweak the outer wired edge of the ribbon to form ripples and waves. Pin into your hat.

1 & 5 Layered Satin Bow

2 & 3 Ruched Ribbon Hat-pin

4 & 6 Wire Mesh Bow

97

STRIPED RIBBON BOATERS

BELOW:

Bashful schoolgirls display their summer straw hats, adorned with single grosgrain ribbons in blue, bubble gum pink and peppermint green.

BELOW RIGHT:

For the smartest of school hats, trim boaters with neat little bows and box pleats.

RIGHT:

A bevy of boaters decorated with stripes of layered grosgrain.

Grosgrain ribbons are the natural embellishments of school hats, blazers and formal attire. Smooth and sturdy, they can stand up to the hazards of melted ice-cream, driving rain or school-bus grime. These thin strips of pistachio green, raspberry pink and turquoise blue are easily stitched to the brim of a hat, magically transforming the scruffy straw into the bedazzling boater.

Keep your decorations plain by wrapping ribbons in single colours around the crown of your boater, or, for a candy-striped effect, try layering grosgrains of different widths on top of one another. Trim the back of the boater with neat little bows or box pleats.

Though generally speaking, the smartest hats are the simplest – black ribbons on black, green on green, mauve on mauve, and so on – straw hats can take a multitude of different ribbons. The textures and colours of straw hats do vary, however, so bear this in mind when designing ribbon trimmings. A rough-textured, plaited hat will look stunning with swathes of plain or dyed raffia, or a cream or beige woven ribbon, tied around the crown. A mixture of ribbons in a natural fibre, such as jute or linen, made into large, looped bows looks good, too. Finer straws in pale buttermilk or pastel colours benefit from more elegant ribbons. Trim them with delicate buds *(see p.115)* of ombré taffeta wire-edge ribbon in the colours of garden roses: pale pink shading into deep purple, egg-yolk yellow fading to pale lemon.

THE RIBBON INDEX

1

2

3

4

5

6

7

8

9

10

11

12

13

14

15

16

FOR KEY *see page 124*

1

2

3

4

5

6

7

8

9

10

11

12

13

14

15

16

17

18

19

20

21

22

23

24

25

26

27

28

29

30

31

32

33

34

35

36

37

38

39

40

FOR KEY *see page 124*

1

2

3

4

5

6

7

8

9

10

11

12

13

14

15

16

17

18

19

28

29

30

31

32

33

34

35

36

37

38

39

40

41

42

43

FOR KEY *see page 124*

1

2

3

4

5

6

7

8

9

10

11

12

13

14

15

23

24

25

26

27

28

29

30

31

32

33

FOR KEY *see page 124*

1

2

3

4

5

6

7

8

9

10

11

12

13

20

21

22

23

24

25

26

27

28

29

30

31

32

33

34

FOR KEY *see page 124*

1

2

3

4

5

6

7

8

9

10

11

12

13

14

21

22

23

24

25

26

27

28

29

30

31

32

33

FOR KEY *see page 124*

TWO SIMPLE BOWS

SINGLE BOW *You will need 50cm/20in of ribbon, with the ends cut into fishtails.*

1 *Lay the ribbon on a flat surface and cross over the two ends like a shawl.*

2 *Pinch together in the centre.*

3 *Tie the pinched centre with florists' wire and pull tight to secure at the back.*

DOUBLE BOW *You will need 1m/1¼yd of ribbon.*

1 *Coil the ribbon on its edge on a flat surface. Make sure both ends finish at 12 o'clock.*

2 *Flatten the loop.*

3 *Pinch the centre of the flattened loop.*

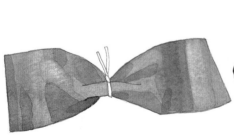

4 *Tie the pinched centre with florists' wire, or a small piece of ribbon, and pull tight to secure at the back.*

5 *Fan out the loops to form a double bow. For a more lavish effect (right), wire a fishtailed ribbon to the back.*

RUCHED FLOWER

RUCHED FLOWER *You will need 1m/1¹/₄yd of wire-edge ribbon.*

1 Lay the ribbon on a flat surface. Take bottom right-hand corner and pull 1cm/¹/₂in of wire from ribbon. Bend wire over.

2 Take bottom left-hand corner of ribbon and pull wire out, ruching ribbon as you go. The ribbon should curl into a horse-shoe shape.

3 Begin rolling ribbon tightly into a bud, keeping the ruched edge at the bottom of the bud. Make five or so turns.

4 Take 5cm/2in of the ribbon and fold it back on itself, then make one turn round the bud. This forms a petal.

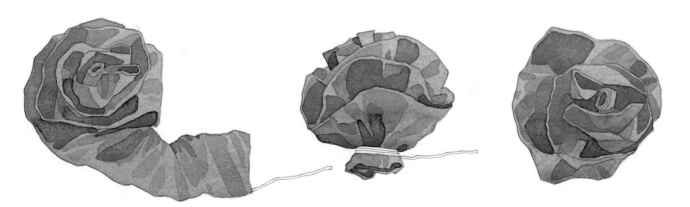

5 Repeat the process until you get to the end of your length of ribbon.

6 Take the loose wire protruding from ribbon and wind it around the base of the flower.

7 Tuck the wire up inside the ribbon flower. Pull out the petals to make a rose shape.

MULTI-LOOP BOW & BUTTERFLY PLEAT

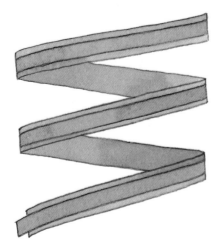

MULTI-LOOP BOW *You will need florists' wire, 2.5m/2³/4yd of 75mm/3in wide ribbon, and the same length of 50mm/2in wide ribbon in a contrasting colour.*

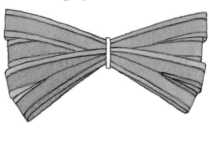

1 Cut a 2m/2¹/4yd length of each ribbon. On a flat surface, lay the thinner ribbon directly on top of the wider one. Keeping the ribbons aligned, start to make folds about 25cm/10in wide, working from side to side.

2 When all the ribbon has been folded, gather up and pinch the middle between the forefinger and thumb of your left hand. Wind florists' wire around the centre and twist tight at the back.

3 Take the remaining 50cm/20in of each ribbon. Lay the thinner ribbon on top of the wider one, and cut neat fishtails in both ribbons at either end. Fold in half and attach to the back of the bow with florists' wire.

BUTTERFLY PLEAT *You will need 25cm/10in of 75mm/3in wide ribbon, and the same length of 38mm/ 1¹/2in wide ribbon in a contrasting colour.*

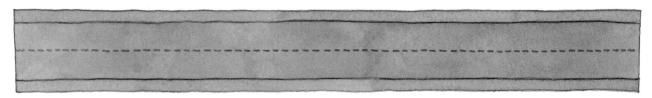

1 On a flat surface, lay the thinner ribbon on top of the wider one and sew the two together by stitching down the centre.

2 Fold over in half. Roughly 30mm/1¹/4in down from the fold, sew horizontally across.
3 Pull out the pleat and lay on a flat surface.
4 Pull the outer edges of the pleat in towards the centre until they meet in the middle.
5 Sew up through the back of the ribbons, catching both pleats at the central join. Finish off neatly at the back.

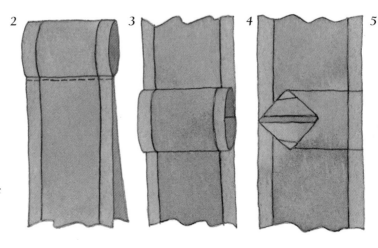

BASIC WEAVING

BASIC WEAVING *To make a weave 50cm/20in square you will need 2.75m/3yd of 100mm/4 in wide ribbon, plus the same in a contrasting colour.*

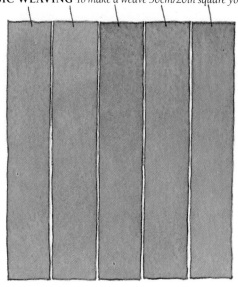

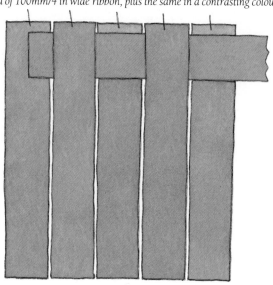

1 Cut the first ribbon into five 55cm/22in strips. Lay them out vertically on a piece of board or thick card so that they are just touching, but not overlapping. Secure at the top with pins.

2 Cut the second ribbon into five 55cm/22in strips. Start to weave the first piece horizontally through the vertical ribbons, taking it over the first, under the second, over the third and so on. When you reach the other side of the board, pin the horizontal ribbon in place at both ends.

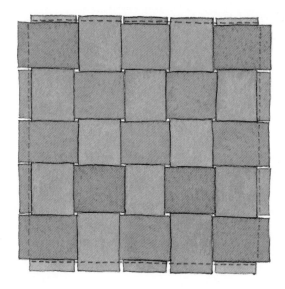

3 Take the second horizontal ribbon and weave it through the vertical ribbons, this time taking it under the first, over the second, and so on. When you reach the other side of the board, push this ribbon up to align neatly against the first horizontal ribbon. Pin in place at both ends.

4 Continue until the square is complete. Make sure all the ribbons align neatly, then pin or tack-stitch in place. To finish off, either sew around the outside, keeping close to the last straight ribbon edges, or bond to a piece of lightweight interfacing using a dry iron on a moderate setting.

FLOWER ROSETTE

FLOWER ROSETTE *You will need 3.5m/3¾yd of woven-edge ribbon.*

1 Cut 1.5m/1¾yd of ribbon and gather-stitch along one outside edge. Pull the thread from one end, to gather the ribbon gently. (If you are using wire-edge ribbon, gather by following the method given on p.115.)

2 Curl the gathered ribbon into a circle and sew the ends together.

3 Repeat steps 1 and 2 using increasingly shorter lengths of ribbon, tack-stitching each new circle inside the one before.

4 Finish the centre by gather-stitching along the outside edge of a 75cm/30in piece of ribbon. Coil the gathered ribbon tightly into a bud and sew down in the centre of the rosette (see right).

VARIATION *Tie a 40cm/16in length of cord into a knot, as shown, then wind one end of the cord around the knot 4 or 5 times. Pull the ends tightly. Sew the knot in the centre of your rosette.*

PETAL ROSETTE

PETAL ROSETTE *You will need 4.7m/5yd of 40mm/1¹/₂in wide wire-edge ribbon.*

1 *First, cut eight 20cm/8in lengths of ribbon. Fold each piece over in half and then sew the ends together as shown.*

2 *On a flat surface, place the eight 'petals' in a ring formation, with the sewn ends just touching. Join the petals together by tack-stiching around the centre of the ring.*

3 *Cut a further eight 20cm/8in lengths of ribbon, and make into petals, as step 1. Place in the centre of the rosette, so that the petals intersect those of the previous layer. Sew in place.*

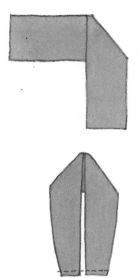

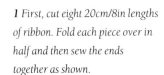

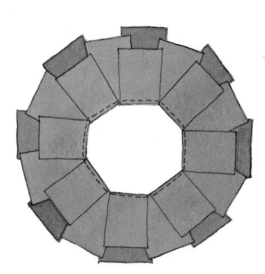

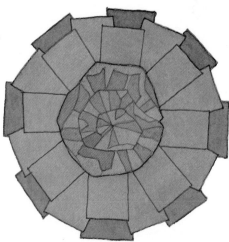

VARIATION
Follow the same method, but use pointed petals, made by folding the ribbon lengths as above, and gather-stitching at the base.

4 *Make up a further eight petals from 15cm/6in lengths of ribbon. Sew in place, with the new petals intersecting those of the previous layer, and aligning with those of the first layer.*

5 *Take the remaining 30cm/12in of wired ribbon and ruche it following steps 1-2 of the Ruched Flower technique given on p.115. Curl the ruched ribbon into a tight circle, tack the ends together and sew down in the centre of your rosette.*

PLAITED RIBBON BRAID & RIBBON WREATH

PLAITED RIBBON BRAID *You will need four 1m/1¹/₄yd lengths of ribbon, of equal width.*

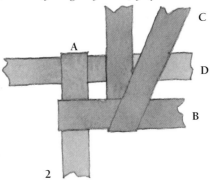

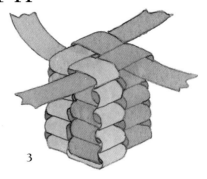

3 *This is one 'turn'. Now make a turn in a clockwise direction. Bring C downwards, fold B back across over the top of C, fold A back up across B, and bring D across A, tucking underneath C. Repeat steps 2 and 3, alternating between anti-clockwise and clockwise turns, until you have a concertina-like shape.*

1 *On a flat surface, lay out the 4 ribbons as shown above, so that they meet in the centre.*
2 *Begin to fold in an anti-clockwise direction.*

Fold A down across D, then B across A and C, and C up over ribbons B and D. Lastly, fold D across the top of C, tucking it underneath A.

4 *Leave 10cm/4in or so of ribbon unfolded at the end. Turn braid upside-down and start the whole process again.*

RIBBON WREATH *You will need a bangle or hoop, a long ribbon to wrap around it, plus two shorter ribbons to wrap around the circumference.*

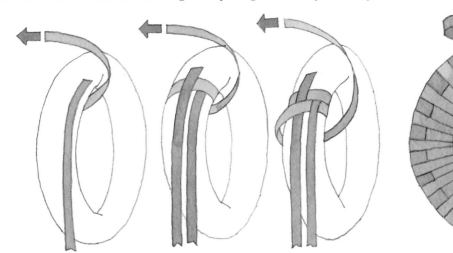

1 *Glue the end of the longer ribbon inside the hoop. Next, glue one of the shorter pieces to the outside, level with the first piece.*

2 *Wind the longer ribbon once around the hoop. Glue the third ribbon above and slightly to the left of the second piece.*

3 *Start to wrap the longer ribbon around the hoop, weaving it alternately over and under the two shorter pieces.*

4 *Continue weaving until the entire hoop is covered, then glue the loose ends of the ribbons to the underside of the hoop.*

TURKS-HEAD KNOT

TURKS-HEAD KNOT *You will need 1.5m/1³/4yd of cord.*

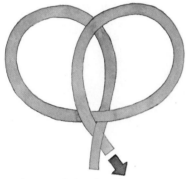

1 Take one end of cord and form into two loops, making sure longer end goes behind shorter one.

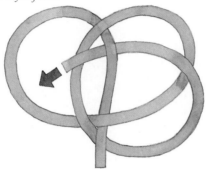

2 Feed the longer, working end through the first loop, back through the middle, then through loop on the left.

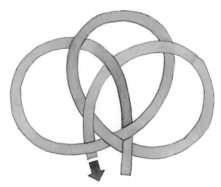

3 Pull full length of the cord through the three holes fairly tightly.

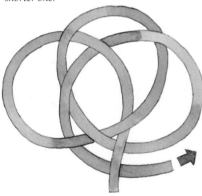

4 You will now have a shape that resembles a carpet beater. At this stage, it helps to turn the knot on its side so you can see where to thread.

5 SIDE VIEW: Hold short end between finger and thumb. Thread working end through knot, to right of, and parallel to, short length.

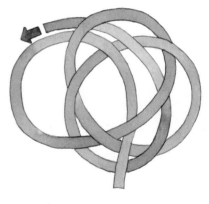

6 Feed entire length of cord through knot, following short length. Move finger and thumb around knot, so you don't lose your place.

7 Keep threading until you end up back at short end. Now follow the next single cord around the knot, keeping just to the right of it.

8 Make third rotation, following the remaining single cord. The knot should now have double loops of cord all the way round.

9 Start process again, following each double loop in turn, until knot fills in. Tuck loose ends of cord inside the gap underneath the knot.

121

TWISTED BOW

TWISTED BOW *You will need 3m/3¹/4yd of wire-edge ribbon, plus two narrower ribbons to bind the centre of the bow.*

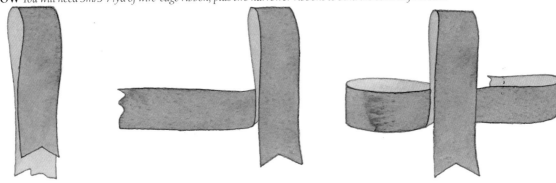

1 *Cut 25cm/10in of wire-edge ribbon and lay to one side. Fishtail ends of longer piece and fold 50cm/20in over at the front.*

2 *Take the longer section and pull out to one side, at right angles to the front section.*

3 *Make a loop 25cm/10in wide, then twist ribbon at the back (see centre) and make a loop of the same size on the opposite side.*

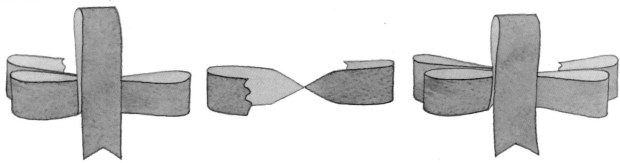

4 *Repeat the process so you have two loops at either side.*

NOTE *Twisting the ribbon at the back of the bow keeps the patterned side of the ribbon visible when you make each new loop.*

5 *Cut off any excess ribbon and glue the end down at the back of the bow.*

6 *Take the 25cm/10in reserved ribbon and cut fishtails at one end. Glue or staple to the back of the bow.*

7 *Lay the narrower ribbons out over the middle of the bow and tie together at the back, to secure the loops and tails in place.*

8 *Gently pull out the loops and tails so that they fan out in different directions.*

WRAP-OVER BOW

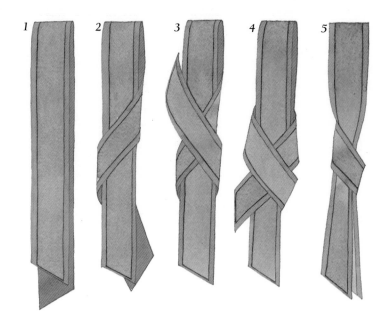

WRAP-OVER BOW *You will need double-sided adhesive tape, 2m/2¹/4yd of 100mm/4in wide ribbon, and the same length of 75mm/3in wide ribbon.*

1 Tape the narrower ribbon down the centre of the wider one. Make diagonal cuts at both ends. Fold over in half, so that the back section is a little longer than the one at the front.

2 Wrap the back section once around the front.

3 Wrap around a second time, taking it up and over the first loop.

4 Now tuck the ribbon end through the loop at the front.

5 Pull both ribbon ends to make a tight knot.

SUPPLIERS

UK

V V Rouleaux
10 Symons Street
London SW3
Tel: 0171 730 3125
Fax: 0171 730 3468
Suppliers of quality ribbons, including Mokuba, Berisford and Julian Faure brands, as well as a wide range of tassels and braids. Ribbons are sold by the metre (minimum order 1 m). Trade discounts given for large orders. If you require further details of any particular ribbon, charts showing full colour ranges are available for a small charge. For prices, phone or fax the above.

AUSTRALIA

For information on nationwide stockists of Berisford ribbons, please contact:
John Birch,
E C Birch Pty Limited,
153 Bridge Road,
Richmond,
Victoria 3121
Tel: 613 419 4944
Fax: 613 419 2148

JAPAN
Mokuba Co Ltd
16-8, Kuramae 4-chome
Taito-Ku
Tokyo 111
Tel: 3 3864 7700
Fax: 3 3864 4013

NEW ZEALAND

For information on nationwide stockists of Berisford ribbons, please contact:
Colin Lowe,
Trendy Trims Limited,
PO Box 13-167,
16-18 George Terrace,
Auckland
Tel: 649 634 4530
Fax: 649 634 6391

SOUTH AFRICA

For information on nationwide stockists of Berisford ribbons, please contact:
Ken Thompson,
Castellane Beltrame
Pty Limited, PO Box
5096, Corner Sheffield
& Brooklyns Road,
East London
Tel: 27 431 312151
Fax: 27 431 312016

USA

For a list of nationwide stockists of Mokuba ribbons, please send a stamped, self-addressed envelope to:
Customer Services,
WFR Ribbon Inc,
259 Center Street,
Phillipsburg,
NJ 08865 3397
Tel: 908 454 7700
Fax: 908 454 0657

* Festive Flag Cake recipe, p.24.
Note for US readers: Rolled fondant icing gives the cake a smooth finish. If you cannot find the ready-to-roll variety, specialist cake stores sell mixes that can be made up.

GLOSSARY KEY

All the ribbons featured in the glossary and throughout the book are available from **V V Rouleaux** or the suppliers listed on p.123. The glossary ribbons can be ordered directly from **V V Rouleaux** (for phone and fax see p.123). When ordering, please quote the reference 'VVCon', followed by the ribbon number given below, and the relevant colour section.

BLACKS & NEUTRALS

1 Mock suede 2 Mock suede 3 Wire-edge velvet 4 Jacquard 5 Appliqué grape 6 Ruched middle organdy 7 Diagonal-pleated satin 8 Printed organdy 9 Woven taffeta 10 Printed satin 11 Jacquard 12 Cotton cord 13 Gold-print organdy 14 Rayon tape 15 Pleated velvet 16 Jacquard 17 Fine silk velvet 18 Metallic stripe velvet 19 Metallic velvet 20 Double-sided picot velvet 21 Picot satin 22 Wire-edge woven 23 Organdy metallic edge 24 Fine jacquard picot 25 Woven tartan 26 Printed satin 27 Picot-edge wired 28 Military jacquard 29 Jacquard

30 Ombré wire-edge 31 Wire mesh metallic 32 Moiré grosgrain 33 Gingham 34 Pleated luminous taffeta 35 Woven metallic 36 Rat tail

PINKS & PURPLES

1 Silk velvet 2 Grosgrain 3 Wire-edge woven 4 Rat tail 5 Pleated satin 6 Pleated velvet 7 Wire-edge print 8 & 9 Jacquard 10 Satin 11 Moiré taffeta satin-edge 12 Wire-edge ombré 13 Wire-edge bee foil print 14 Wire-edge ombré 15 Wire-edge woven 16 Luminous taffeta 17 Gingham 18 Shot organdy 19 Luminous taffeta 20 Gingham 21 Pleated shot organdy 22 Silk 23 Jacquard 24 Ruched satin 25 Metallic bead yarn 26 Wire edge 27 Bolduc 28 Bolduc 29 Overlock pure silk 30 Taffeta jacquard-edge 31 Fine silk 32 Fine silk 33 Luminous shot 34 Wire-edge taffeta 35 Velvet 36 Moiré grosgrain 37 Organdy 38 Jacquard 39 Rayon tape 40 Georgette satin-edge

BLUES

1 Military tie braid 2 Military tie braid 3 Box-pleat grosgrain 4 Frilled satin 5 Diagonal-pleat satin 6 Boat jacquard 7 Woven stripe organdy 8 Printed organdy 9 Woven wired metallic 10 Appliqué organdy 11 Satin-edge georgette 12 Frill-edge taffeta 13 Printed satin 14 Wire-edge printed 15 Jacquard metallic 16 Shot moiré grosgrain 17 Woven chequerboard 18 Appliqué grosgrain 19 Double-sided luminous brushed 20 Cotton tape 21 Woven satin stripe 22 Metallic glitter wire-edge 23 Wire-edge check 24 Printed wire-edge 25 Jacquard 26 Luminous taffeta 27 Printed satin 28 Jacquard 29 Woven tartan 30 Jacquard 31 Gingham 32 Luminous shot 33 Jacquard 34 Velvet matt-edge 35 Silk velvet 36 Shot velvet 37 Woven tartan 38 Jacquard 39 Woven cotton tape 40 Wire-edge woven 41, 42 & 43 Satin

YELLOWS, ORANGES & BROWNS

1 Grosgrain 2 Cotton tape 3 Cotton tape 4 Jacquard 5 Organdy metallic-edge 6 Military tie braid 7 Knitted tape 8 Wire-edge printed 9 Crazy-pleat georgette 10 Check velvet 11 Wire-edge printed 12 Wire edge 13 Jacquard 14 Wire edge 15 Double-sided picot 16 Gingham 17 Silk velvet 18 Stripe velvet 19 Plush silk velvet 20 Satin-backed velvet 21 Mock suede 22 Wired ombré 23 Organdy 24 Wired ombré 25 Wired ombré 26 Jacquard 27 Jacquard 28 Jacquard 29 Flocked taffeta 30 Jacquard 31 Wired woven metallic 32 Jacquard 33 Wired gingham

GREENS

1 Woven tartan 2 Nylon woven 3 Wired cut-edge 4 Velvet stripe 5 Wired cut-edge 6 Picot grosgrain 7 Pleated luminous taffeta 8 Velvet frill edge 9 Wire-edge woven 10 Organdy woven 11 Wire edge 12 Ruched gingham 13 Grosgrain 14 Cut-edge craft 15 Satin-edge taffeta 16 Wired jacquard 17 Jacquard picot 18 Wire edge 19 Organdy 20 Jacquard 21 Rose buds

22 Jacquard 23 Double-sided brushed luminous 24 Satin 25 Woven purl-edge 26 Check gingham 27 Mole braid 28 Jacquard 29 Pleated satin 30 Wire-edge 31 Ruched satin 32 Check gingham 33 Wire-edge 34 Double-sided velvet

REDS

1 Organdy printed 2 Cut-edge wired shot 3 Cotton tape 4 Shot pleated organdy 5 Appliquéd satin 6 Cut-edge wired printed 7 Cut-edge wired 8 Cut-edge moiré 9 Wire-edge jacquard 10 Wire-edge metallic print 11 Wire-edge printed 12 Wire-edge woven shot 13 Organdy metallic edge 14 Piping velvet 15 Printed mock suede 16 Shot organdy 17 Jacquard purl-edge 18 Wire-edge printed 19 Shot velvet 20 Metallic woven 21 Picot-edge organdy 22 Wire edge 23 Wire-edge woven 24 Jacquard 25 Printed gingham 26 Gingham 27 Woven tartan 28 Nylon woven jacquard 29 Check velvet 30 Metallic-edge satin 31 Wire-edge stripe 32 Woven tartan 33 Woven elastic

ACKNOWLEDGEMENTS

With special thanks to Mokuba Co. Ltd who kindly supplied ribbons for photography and without whose generous support this book would not have been possible. Mokuba ribbons are available through VV Rouleaux, or through the stockists listed on p.123.

Thanks also to Berisford Ribbons for supplying ribbons for photography.

The author would like to thank Tom and Margaret Lewis (Grumpypops and Danny), John and Fiona Armstrong, Tim, Sylvia and Ettie Stevens, Florence Brooks, Charlotte Guthrie, Jessica and Katie King and Oscar.
Thanks also to Emma Davison (hats, pp.94-7), Virginia Nichols of Michael John Management (tel: 0171 409 2706 – hair styling, pp.44-5), Suzanne Ruggles, Basia Zarzycka (tel: 0171 351 7276 – ribbon flowers, pp.6-7 and ribbon bags, p.76-7), Sue Thompson (bed linen, pp.68-71), Kate Wilson (tel: 01273 486 718 – book binding, pp.102-13), Sonya Sibbons (cake recipe, p.24), the Garden House school for the loan of school uniforms, Simone Bendex, Carl Sandeman, Karin Woodruff, and Sally Harding.

And finally, special thanks to Pia, Georgina and Julia, and the staff at V V Rouleaux –

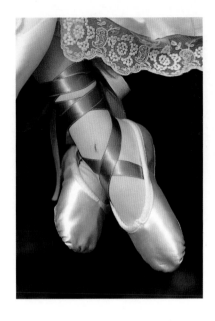

Prue, Andrea and Chris – for their help and support, and to Becky Metcalf for first giving me the idea for the book.

PICTURE ACKNOWLEDGEMENTS

The publishers would like to thank the following organizations for their kind permission to reproduce the following images: **8** *Bridgeman Art Library (National Gallery, London);* **9** *Bridgeman Art Library;* **10** *top and bottom Angelo Hornak (courtesy of The National Maritime Museum, Greenwich) ;* **10** *centre Bridgeman Art Library (Royal Hospital Chelsea);* **11** *Giraudon/Bridgeman Art Library (Chateau de Versailles).*
The following photographs were specially taken for Conran Octopus by Patrick McLeavey: 15, 102-13.

The publishers would like to thank the following for providing props for photography:

GREEN & STONE
259 Kings Road,
London SW3 5E2
Tel: 0171 352 6521
Ink pot and pencils, pp.21-3

INDIGO
275 New Kings Road,
London SW6 4RD
Tel: 0171 384 310
Baubles, p.48

PAPERCHASE
213 Tottenham Court Road,
London W1P 9AF
Tel: 0171 580 8496
Boxes and wrapping papers, pp.30-1

THE WATER MONOPOLY
16-18 Lonsdale Road, London NW6
Tel: 0171 624 2636
Bathtub, pp.72-3

YOUNG ENGLAND CHILDRENSWEAR
47 Elizabeth Street,
London SW1
Tel: 0171 259 9003
Phoebe's dress. p.50

INDEX